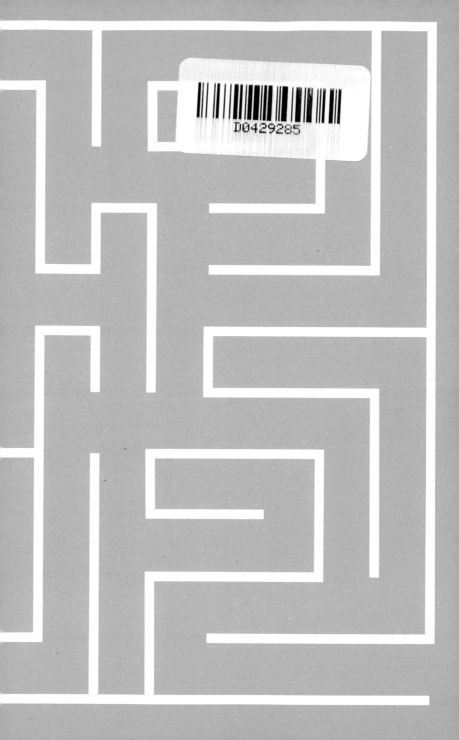

YOU
ARE
A
GLOBAL
CITIZEN

_____'s journal

Teach®
Yourself

YOU ARE A GLOBAL CITIZEN

A GUIDED JOURNAL FOR THE
CULTURALLY CURIOUS

by Damon Dominique

First published by Teach Yourself in 2023
An imprint of John Murray Press
A division of Hodder & Stoughton Ltd,
An Hachette UK company

1

A CIP catalogue record for this title is available from the British Library

Hardback ISBN 978 1 529 38994 4
eBook ISBN 978 1 529 38995 1

Typeset by KnowledgeWorks Global Ltd.

Printed and bound in Great Britain by Clays Ltd, Elcograf S.p.A.

John Murray Press policy is to use papers that are natural, renewable
and recyclable products and made from wood grown in sustainable forests.
The logging and manufacturing processes are expected to conform to the
environmental regulations of the country of origin.

John Murray Press	Nicholas Brealey Publishing
Carmelite House	Hachette Book Group
50 Victoria Embankment	Market Place, Center 53, State Street
London EC4Y 0DZ	Boston, MA 02109, USA

www.teachyourself.com

Contents

ORIGINS

INTERNAL

EXTERNAL

About the author

DAMON DOMINIQUE was born to be a nomad - after all, it's Damon spelled backwards.

Best known for his eccentric, whimsical travel videos and rebellious, philosophical nature, Damon Dominique is a global travel personality who has documented his comedic and cultural adventures fluently in over five languages, in over 50 countries, and in over 500 travel videos on his popular You Tube channel @damondominique, establishing himself amongst the social media generation as *the* international and multilingual voice in travel.

He has topped the list of *Forbes* Top Travel Influencers and been featured in publications including *The Washington Post* and *Mashable.*

A note from Damon

ON PAPER, my nationality would tell you I belong to one country in particular, but in my mind, I always knew my identity was not confined by international borders. So in the name of curating this global citizenship I had always seen for myself, I spent years navigating visa limits, dabbling in foreign tongues, and purposely traveling to countries I didn't know the first thing about. Understandably, these experiences around the world have led me to many exciting and uncomfortable unknowns: I've landed in Tokyo Narita airport and realized only at border control that I had left my passport back in the Beijing airport; I've visited more doctors and pharmacies outside of the USA than in the USA for everything from Montezuma's revenge to an uncontrollable rash I developed after swimming in a Thai waterfall; and I've been through just about every French administration runaround trying to navigate life as an American expat. But no matter what happened, or continues to happen, these experiences were as unpredictable as they were impactful, and most of all, they were the experiences I had always been looking for. I wasn't satisfied with an education about the world; I wanted an education around the world. That's why I wrote this book about the steps and questions that got me there - because I see it for you too.

Damon Danji

Introduction

YOU ARE a global citizen.

Yes, you.

You, someone who just stopped in the airport bookstore to buy a pack of overpriced peanuts and instead found themselves mindlessly picking this up. You, someone who was gifted this book because you once vaguely mentioned that one thing that one time in that one place about wanting to see the world. You, a citizen of your country, who has maybe never even questioned anything about your own culture at all. In fact, especially you.

At this very moment, you and everyone around you (and not around you) are where you are based upon a set of rigid rules in society that dictate who can be where, when, and why. Some of us never have to consider these rules— content enough with our place in the world and enjoying where we're from—while others are constantly questioning their cultural status quo and applying for every last visa to get anywhere but where they are.

If you're reading this, it's likely that you fall into this last category, so to start with, it's important to recognize that we owe a lot to where we were born, and yet it's a stroke of chance that has shaped everything from the rights we have, to the image others around the world already have of us, to what we have grown to like. Because, to some extent, these aspects of ourselves were defined for us, and not by us, it would be unwise to hold to them with such conviction. Maybe your favorite song exists in Romanian, but you've never heard it. Maybe you haven't yet tried your favorite food because you haven't yet encountered a Brazilian chef. Maybe the country of Denmark aligns more with your beliefs on how a society should function, but you've just never learned much about it. This doesn't mean you have to sprint around the world trying every last thing in every last place; rather, it's the simple recognition that all of your current favorites were once firsts.

Had you been born halfway across the world and presented another set of cultural norms, you could have very well adopted those and made them your favorites, and this is why the first step in becoming a global citizen is to always maintain a childlike wonder about the world around you. The second is to understand that the entire reason you are now aware of the preferences in the culture you did adopt is because at one point you were curious about life's happenings around you and willing enough to risk not liking something for the sake of liking something. As you have moved through life, you may have maintained this open mindset about the unknown, or denied it, already having made up your mind about how you'd like life to carry on. We can look around today and see who is still in each stage—those who are enthusiastic to explore what's new, unknown, and different, and those who are reluctant to deviate beyond the nationality script that was provided for them at birth.

It's now time to go on a journey and question all the ways your culture has made you into the person you are as you skim this very sentence. And for this journey, you won't need your passport.

Why this book right now

IT IS often through discovering other cultures—whether halfway across the globe or halfway down the street—that we can better understand who we are, and how the culture, or cultures, we are from have shaped us.

If we were to zoom out from Earth, we would quickly realize that our national borders are invented constructs—and thus, so are the manmade divisions between us: our home country's social codes, political climate, status in the world, and even the jokes sometimes made about other countries in the latest comedy film, all influence how we see the world, and how others halfway across the world see us. We often blindly take on this conditioning from the culture we grew up in and operate in a global world from it. Eight billion people around the world will do the same with another preferred cultural default.

In fact, for a large part of the world, it could be argued that some humans, by no fault of their own, currently live in a state of relative cultural ignorance. We may be able to mutter a few words in Spanish, point to Greece on a map, or recognize the sound of a British accent, but until we've got our ID card, or paid our government the price of a passport (and convinced another that we are worthy of a visit, or a stay with a visa), we are confined to one's land, its culture, and its people.

With the invention of the Internet, the world is becoming increasingly connected, globalized, and yet increasingly divided. We need such a book to help us to become more self-aware and observant of how and where our cultures are at play in our own thinking and behavior (and where they are for others), so that we can think beyond the borders of our minds and countries, and enable us to understand how we see the world and why.

Understanding why we are the way we are, and why others are the way they are is key in moving society forward in a peaceful, evolved way - because whether we know it yet or not, before any other label, we are all *global citizens.*

How to use this book

YOU ARE *A Global Citizen* is divided into three sections. "Origins" consists of everything that was decided for you before you got here and the facets of the past you can no longer change. "Internal" consists of more abstract concepts with which our relationships aren't so obvious. "External" consists of tangible and ever-changing experiences in the world that also influence the person you become. Each section contains six chapters enabling you to delve into the detail of each theme presented.

The exercises in this book should be done in private. Examining your identity and culture requires a level of vulnerability, reflection, and thoughtfulness about where you currently stand behind the façade. Set some time aside for yourself to work on the questions away from your typical surroundings and any distractions, to be able to truly get in touch with the you that exists beyond external influences.

This book has no right or wrong responses. This is your book, and you should feel free to answer the questions however you wish. The important thing is to answer the questions authentically for you, rather than what you think you should answer based on other people's opinions.

This book should take time. Maybe you're looking for your place in the world, or maybe you feel comfortable but would like to explore even deeper. In either case, this isn't a book with a deadline or obvious end point. If you're struggling to provide a meaningful response to one of the questions, skip it and revisit it later

Working through this book under these parameters will not only benefit you, but also the people you spend time with now and the people you will meet in the future. Your level of self-knowledge affects everyone else in your life; indeed, you only meet others as deeply as you've met yourself.

First reflections

WE'LL BEGIN and end this workbook in the same way: with a set of questions used to establish where your cultural values, beliefs, and identity stand as of now, and finally, where they stand when they will have been more clearly defined.

Based on what you currently know, what aspects of your culture do you embody?

_____

_____

_____

_____

_____

How much does the rest of the world know about your culture?

_____

_____

_____

_____

_____

How do you think the rest of the world views your country?

_____

_____

_____

_____

_____

How identified are you currently with your country? How many other countries' national anthems, flags, or government officials could you identify?

_____

_____

Do you know your country's history from any other country's perspective?

What regions of the world have you been told to avoid? Would those same regions have been told to avoid your country?

Note any other initial observations about your country or culture before we get started:

1
ORIGINS

HOW CAN WE KNOW WHO IS THE OTHER UNTIL WE KNOW WHO IS THE SELF?

—Terence McKenna

THERE ARE two truths we need to expose right away: First, we don't choose to be born. Second, we don't choose *where* to be born. For some, it's quite a cruel ruling of fate, whereas, for others, the odds are ever in their favor. This seems to work just fine for some people, but for those who are drawn to a book like this in the first place, we're intrigued enough to peel back the layers and discover the roots of this *here* and *there*, and all the things that are neither here nor there. We don't want to simply be determined by the culture we inherited, without at least investigating the who, what, where, when, and why.

In the "Origins" section we're digging up our roots and looking at where it, we, all began. We start with the **Hometown** chapter, which offers us a refreshing lens through which to explore the unique place we called home. We then dissect our first relationships in the world, with our **Family**, which go on to influence our understandings of how the rest of our relationships should look. Next, we examine **Language**, the very stepping stone that underpins our ability to communicate any of these ideas in the first place. In the **Education** chapter, we dive into where our interests came from in the first place and how they may have been shaped by our country's educational system alone. Then, we notice the various aspects of our identity that remain rather invisible until we learn to see ourselves outside the context of the **Nationality** we were born into. Finally, we look into how our views on **Race and ethnicity** might impact our views of not only ourselves but the world around us.

Exactly how you turned out could be your doing, your family's doing, or your culture's doing. After all, these three are happening in the same place, intertwined all at once. The end result is always the same: You didn't choose your initial environment and yet you're a product of it. How so? Well ...

Hometown

IT'S CALL time, the curtain swings up, and action: You're born. Born into the backdrop of a hometown which will act as a theater set with you at center stage. How are the characters interacting with each other? In which accent are they speaking? What are their backstories? Who designed this set? And how were you cast in the lead role in a production whose cold-read audition you can't even remember signing up for?

This first backdrop of your life is chosen by your family, and whether a conscious choice on their behalf or mere circumstance, the hometown in which you grow up has a ripple effect on what choices you then make for yourself.

I grew up in Indiana, and so did my parents, and so did their parents. More specifically, I grew up in Glenridge Manor, which sounds quite fancy for a 300-lot trailer park. Despite my enjoyable childhood, small-town America made me feel uninteresting, uninspiring, and, fitting to the name, small. Although I felt different from my family in this aspect, who seemed to not only feel zero FOMO they weren't in some bustling, cosmopolitan city, but also preferred to stay out of one, it wasn't until I was 20 and my boyfriend from France flew in to meet my family that I began to see Midwest America as its own destination rather than a place I "unfortunately" ended up. Throughout my entire life, I believed that life was happening elsewhere; it had never dawned on me that where I was from could be that *elsewhere* someone, somewhere, was curious about.

Time and again, we become accustomed to what it is about our hometowns that makes them unique. Essentially, we operate on autopilot, blind to all the ways we might sing along to the unique, local radio station jingles or all agree on the best place to grab Sunday brunch, when, in fact, these aren't obvious to someone passing through town. While I saw my hometown in terms of which shortcuts to take to cut cross-town, which gas station had the best fountain soda, and where to enroll in summer tennis lessons, my then-boyfriend noticed all of the town's cultural quirks: yellow school buses from the movies, retro diners where servers spoke with a slight Midwestern twang, and children carrying their quad skates into the roller rink—things I had never even realized made up my entire small-town American childhood, let alone shaped me into the person he had found interesting in the first place.

Your hometown, no matter where it is, how famous it is, or how much pride or resentment you feel toward it, represents both a unique location in the world and a distinct reference point from which you operate from daily.

There, literally, is no place like home.

CHECK-IN

- How many generations of your family have lived in your hometown? With whom did it start?

- What is the reason most people choose to live in your hometown in the first place?

- Is your hometown a destination others know about?

- Where would you have rather spent your childhood?

- Did the majority of people you grew up around live a similar or a different lifestyle to each other?

YOU ARE HERE

1. To what extent are you aware of the origins and history of your hometown?

Try to find out about how your hometown was founded. How has your hometown impacted your identity? How could your identity have developed differently had this history gone another way?

_____

_____

_____

_____

_____

_____

_____

_____

2. A psychic tells you you'll spend the rest of your life in your hometown. Describe your initial reaction with a few adjectives:

_____

_____

_____

_____

_____

_____

_____

_____

3. Draw a map of the neighborhood you grew up in. Fill it in with your neighbors. How well do/did you know them? Think about each of these individuals and how they impacted you and your identity.

4. What was the reputation of your neighborhood, school, hometown, and general region? How did this affect what you thought of your surroundings and, by extension, your identity?

Were you from a small town or booming metropolis? Were you from the nicer part of town or the not-so-nice part of town?

_____

_____

_____

_____

_____

_____

_____

_____

5. You're asked by a travel magazine to capture your hometown's beauty in four photos. Where or of what would you take your photos? What do you think these say about what you value?

_____

_____

_____

_____

_____

_____

_____

_____

_____

_____

6. What types of job opportunities might you always be able to find in your hometown? Are they fitting for you?

_____

_____

_____

_____

_____

_____

_____

_____

_____

_____

7. You have a friend coming to visit your hometown. What do you show them? What culture(s) are represented? Are there places that you have not yet been to?

_____

_____

_____

_____

_____

_____

_____

_____

_____

_____

8. An exchange student just moved to your hometown. What quirks might they notice that you may have grown accustomed to?

_____

_____

_____

_____

_____

_____

_____

_____

_____

_____

9. Shade in this drawing of a person with how much you feel like yourself when in your hometown.

Is your family an accurate representation of your hometown's culture?

10. In the columns, explain why your hometown is a good and bad place to grow up:

Good place	Bad place

Family

ON TO more things you didn't get to choose: your family. From day one, you're thrust into well-established rituals, rulebooks, and routines which go on to shape your first understandings of what is "normal" in terms of human interaction and relationships: which parent/guardian will likely console you after a bad day at school, how often distant cousins speak to each other, and whether your family finds it funny or disgraceful that your uncle is drunk at your Saturday afternoon soccer match. In other words, the identity you initially take on is partly defined by your family's past good and bad life experiences before you're even born—experiences that taught them to behave the way they do, which then teach you to behave the way you do.

As we move through life and are placed in contexts outside of our families—school, work, and trips to other places around the world—we encounter others with equally as juicy and developed family backstories, and by comparison, we quickly learn the ways in which we'd like to confidently carry on being the next extension to our family name and the aspects we'd like to quietly discard.

My first glimpse of a life outside the context of my family was at age 16. I had convinced my parents to let me use the money I earned from my part-time barista job to spend the summer studying Spanish at a Barcelona language school: *"Well, son, it's your money after all."* In this way, my American parents were very American, placing a heavy emphasis on the freedom of the individual—that you have the autonomy to make your own decisions as long as you're ready to take responsibility and live with the consequences. Though my first week in Barcelona was spent reveling in the novelty of a foreign country so far removed from anything I had ever known—10 p.m. tapas, flashy nightclubs, and beach volleyball—by week two I found myself homesick and sending daily emails to my mom.

There's nothing more sobering than traveling halfway across the world and living within a context where nobody even knows your family exists, unlike at home where your school teachers remember your siblings, your barista knows your family order, and your neighbors know which house you belong to. On the contrary, they've never seen your family, never heard your family, and never heard *about* your family. While liberating in the sense that you've got a newfound anonymity without any expectations or reputation to hold up, ultimately, it's a situation that asks the existential question "Who are you? What are you all about?" And for a 16-year-old who had never considered himself as a standalone person, let alone who had never heard the word "existential," it was bound to be a pivotal turning point in my, or anyone's, life.

As the summer carried on changing me, so too did the tone of my Facebook posts: from counting down the days until I could go home to counting down the days until I had to go home. I was finally grasping what it was that makes anyone homesick: I had been approaching my experience abroad from the point of view of my American family's preferred way of doing things rather than approaching it from the point of view of my Spanish host family who had grown up there, loved every bit of it, and preferred the culture to mine.

It often takes an unfamiliar context like this to understand the familiar one that involves our families. Having lived with a host family for eight long weeks, I was finally able to see my family for who they were, to see myself as a part of them, and finally to see myself and my own life apart from them. A changed 16-year-old, I went home to Indiana feeling confident with the new realization that no matter where I go around the world from there, *su casa* can always be *mi casa*.

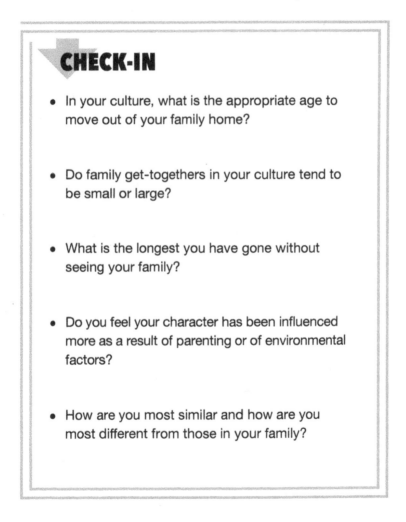

CHECK-IN

- In your culture, what is the appropriate age to move out of your family home?

- Do family get-togethers in your culture tend to be small or large?

- What is the longest you have gone without seeing your family?

- Do you feel your character has been influenced more as a result of parenting or of environmental factors?

- How are you most similar and how are you most different from those in your family?

YOU ARE HERE

1. Draw your family tree. How far back are you currently aware of your family's ancestry?

What most interests you about your genealogy and your family's lives before your birth?

2. Imagine your wedding. You can only invite a select number of people. Make the list.

Was that list filled more with friends or family? Would your family expect you to invite your distant relatives?

3. You're starting a family. In the columns below, place the characteristics, traditions, and routines of your own family that you would like to keep, as well as those you would like you to do away with.

Characteristics	Traditions	Routines

4. If you and your parents were the same age, would you be friends?

In which ways do you get along with your parents (or not)? What are your shared values? Are your parents still playing the role of the parent, or are these roles changing as you get older? Do you feel you influence your parents in the same way they have influenced you?

5. How would people describe your family?

Do the people who live near you today know your family? To what extent? Does this influence your day-to-day behavior (keeping up a reputation, or not feeling the obligation to, for example)?

_____

_____

_____

_____

_____

_____

_____

_____

6. If your family was dropped in a foreign country, how well would they fare? Who would be the most and least adaptable?

_____

_____

_____

_____

_____

_____

_____

_____

_____

_____

7. Consider any adversities your family has had to overcome. How did these affect your family dynamic? For example, family members who made off-putting remarks, moving abroad, a loss in the family.

_____

_____

_____

_____

_____

_____

_____

_____

_____

_____

8. What are, or would be, your faults as a parent?

Is your culture known for strict parenting, or a more laid-back, laissez-faire *approach?*

_____

_____

_____

_____

_____

_____

_____

_____

_____

_____

9. You're in your prime, working in your dream career and living life abroad as a global citizen, when suddenly your family needs your help and requests you move back home. What do you do?

How much does your family count on and rely on you? How easy is it for you to take off, away from your family? How might living away from your family affect your relationship?

_____

_____

_____

_____

_____

_____

_____

_____

10. On the timeline below, loosely plan the next 30 years of your life.

How much was family considered? Were there kids involved? Was your relationship with your parents considered? Where did these 30 years take place? What does this show you about how you want your life to look?

Language

LANGUAGE IS the most basic building block of communication, the origin of all other origins—before everything else can get done, whether computer science or cosmetology, we need to understand first how to understand. To put it simply, we're all essentially moving about our day communicating in beeps, boops, and bops—a series of agreed-upon letters and sounds streamed together to convey meaning. Even as you read this, you might be imagining a set of signs and sounds paired together to understand what is on the page. String together another set of bips, beps, and bups, and if you haven't extensively studied that language pattern, you won't understand, even though those bips, beps, and bups are just as irrelevant to the object in question.

You see, reality itself has no language; humans created languages in order to effectively communicate with one another. We can notice this by standing between a French speaker and an English speaker who are both looking at the same object, such as this very book, for example. One says *livre*, while the other says *book*. The object itself is not innately a "book," nor a "livre." It just *is*.

Essentially what we're doing is breaking down the existence of language, while using the same language to do so. Repeat "book" 20 times over and it would eventually lose all meaning and make you wonder why the medieval English chose *that* sound combination for the word. When we multiply that linguistic breakdown by the hundreds of thousands of words in our language, then realize our thoughts are operating in the confines of language, we can look at those confines and consider the highly contested Sapir–Whorf hypothesis, which states that an individual's worldview is influenced by the language they speak. For example:

- Is it just a mere coincidence that when presented with a hilarious joke, nice apartment view, or gorgeous piece of artwork my Parisian friends' go-to is almost always a seemingly unimpressed *pas mal* (not bad), whereas my English-speaking friends go straight to an animated *awesome* and *amazing*? Does this say something deeper about our default standards?
- Some languages have varying ways in which people address each other. Do those that have an informal and formal *you* system categorize strangers differently? Respect them more? Or does one general *you* mean we're more likely to see each other as equals—no matter one's status or age?
- Our relationships to our own desires may also be affected. Do languages that don't use the verb "to have" see materialism in another way? Do languages that don't use the verb "to be" feel less attached to a specific identity?
- Even the vocabulary available to us in our languages can shape our articulateness. Do languages that have various words for the various forms of love (romantic, sexual, familial, platonic, etc.) feel love on a deeper level? On a similar note, we can see how some languages explain things in a more efficient way. For instance, we'll often borrow words from other languages where ours is lacking. *Déjà vu* in French, for example, translates to *already seen* and is a quick way to understand what is meant by the sensation of feeling like you've lived this exact moment already.

Our respective native languages are full of these, and depending on the pop culture, slang, or technological advancements at the time, new vocabulary and therefore new ways to express ourselves are constantly being added to our speech.

As we see, many people learn languages to acquire a skill set in order to connect with large groups of people with different worldviews that we would have otherwise missed out on. Studying another language, or even our own, makes us reconsider the way we've made sense of reality thus far.

It's literally not *what* you say, it's *how* you say it.

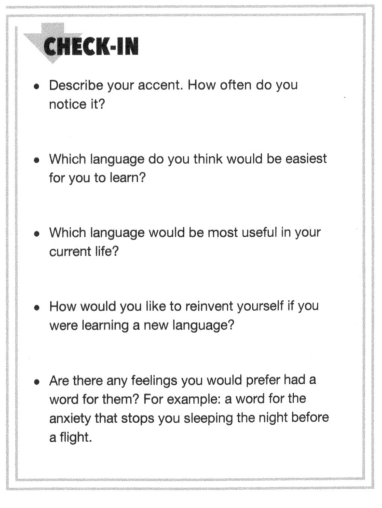

CHECK-IN

- Describe your accent. How often do you notice it?

- Which language do you think would be easiest for you to learn?

- Which language would be most useful in your current life?

- How would you like to reinvent yourself if you were learning a new language?

- Are there any feelings you would prefer had a word for them? For example: a word for the anxiety that stops you sleeping the night before a flight.

YOU ARE HERE

1. List the regions around the world you can travel to without having to know a new language. Do you feel a certain alliance or affinity with those nations whose inhabitants speak the same language as you? For example: the UK, USA and Australia; Spain and Mexico; Brazil and Portugal.

2. How is your regional accent perceived in your country?

Do you feel proud about it? Or try to restrain it in front of others with other accents? Which ones? Have you ever changed your accent depending on where you are?

3. Draw a hierarchy of how you perceive accents that you've come across.

Are there accents you find more sexy, charming, intelligent, and others that you'd use when making a joke? What does this say about your region's or country's relationship to those places? How does this impact your perception of the speakers of these languages?

4. You're creating a skit about people from your region or country. What expressions are common and would you be sure to include? For example: expressions your parents taught you, slang terms you use with friends.

Can you draw any conclusions about how this framed your own thinking? For example: "If you don't have anything nice to say, then don't say anything at all." Are there words or expressions that only those from your region use?

5. How well could you teach someone your native language?

How much are you aware of how your own language works? Are you aware of specific grammar rules, verb conjugations, exceptions to rules, and so on?

_____

_____

_____

_____

_____

_____

_____

_____

_____

_____

6. You use a "big" word. What would your inner circle make of this? Would they be intrigued or find it pretentious?

Who around you has the highest level of vocabulary, or speaks the most formally? Do you find yourself modifying your language depending on who you're speaking to? How?

_____

_____

_____

_____

_____

_____

_____

_____

_____

7. For the convenience of tourism, your city is voting on translating street signs, restaurant menus, and store names from your native language to the global language. Would you support or oppose this kind of globalization? Why? What do you think of English as a global language? What impact does this have on tourism and local languages?

How hard should we try to preserve languages with smaller numbers of speakers? Would choosing an invented language like Esperanto be a more considerate than one that has existed for centuries like English? Is there a growing dominance of another language in your culture?

_____

_____

_____

_____

_____

_____

_____

8. What privileges and disadvantages does your native language offer you in the world?

How far does your native language stretch in the world? Can you catch a movie abroad, find a book in a bookstore, read a restaurant menu, understand all the song lyrics in a club?

_____

_____

_____

_____

_____

_____

_____

9. Your presence is requested to work at a foreign embassy where all correspondence will be in a language other than English. Which language would you start studying?

Why do you want to learn the language you want to learn? Have you studied any other languages? If so, which? Was this voluntary or compulsory?

10. You meet someone, whether a friend or love interest, and feel an undeniable connection, but you don't speak the same language. Now what?

Do you learn their language? Do you use Google Translate for the entire relationship? Do you let the idea of this budding connection fade away?

Education

WHAT YOU'RE learning in this book is to unlearn everything you've ever learned. So, grab your pen and paper, and let's educate ourselves about our own traditional education systems.

In the USA, for example, public schools are funded by the taxes of each district's residents. The first point to consider is what percentage of these taxes will be set aside for education. The second is what percentage each school in the district receives. These funds are reallocated to the varying school districts based on a number of factors that will differ among local governments and from country to country. The obvious ones are enrollment size, average number of students in a classroom per teacher, and increased demands like English as a second language classes, special education, or the need for a performing arts school. It's this funding that determines everything from where district lines were drawn that sent you to your school to what kind of support and which subjects you were offered once you got there—all of which go on to influence your academic interests and overall success.

The type of subjects and type of teachers teaching them play the biggest role of all: my school's French enrollment numbers exploded the day our school hired a gorgeous French teacher and students were never more eager to try out their "Voulez-vous coucher avec moi" line. Nonetheless, the world as a whole got smarter that day.

Speaking of French, it was only during my academic year abroad in France that it hit me that the history of the USA I had learned my entire life was ... entirely from the US perspective. As is likely the case with every country when they teach their own history, my country was always positioned as the good guys with the good solutions. In my education, we had never been encouraged to challenge our country, but to stand by it. It's not that this version of history is false; it's just that it's alarming to never have been exposed to another version of the past until I enrolled in that *Civilisation américaine* class.

Our professor was a classy Frenchman who had previously taught at a Kansas high school. He made all kinds of intriguing observations—how American small talk is charming but, to him, superficial and how odd it was that in many of our pharmacies you could also buy cigarettes and alcohol. He later taught us how the way we view history is influenced by which side of the story you're learning it from. For instance, the Revolutionary War in the USA is known as the American War of Independence in the UK—even the names themselves carry different weight. It's the same war, but one that's highlighted in American history, where the battle played a monumental role in the country's founding, but barely mentioned at all in British history lessons. It baffled me that we could all be operating in the same world with different stories about the past, which in return, influence how we see each other in the present.

As we sat in that classroom learning American history from a French perspective, perhaps it was more obvious to those French speakers, where *history* and *story* are the same word (*l'histoire*), that not all history is a mutual agreement on the story of the past. In the same way that you and I may purposely leave out, paraphrase, or emphasize parts of our own carefully crafted narrative, what we're taught about our country's history is ultimately up to the length of our textbooks and the moments our countries choose to include.

Of course, facts cannot be denied and although we're all trying our best to educate ourselves, we're doing so around the world with different books on required reading lists, varying subjects in core curricula, and ever-changing requirements of what even makes it onto teachers' syllabi. This should be proof enough that being the best version of a global citizen is realizing that no matter who is in front of you at any given moment, they will always know something you don't, and thus can always be your teacher.

Class dismissed.

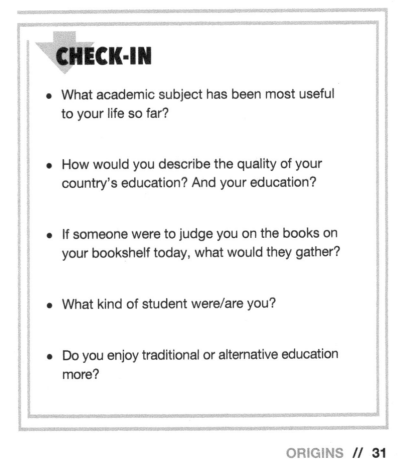

CHECK-IN

- What academic subject has been most useful to your life so far?

- How would you describe the quality of your country's education? And your education?

- If someone were to judge you on the books on your bookshelf today, what would they gather?

- What kind of student were/are you?

- Do you enjoy traditional or alternative education more?

YOU ARE HERE

1. What are you currently learning about? How does this make you feel?

In what ways are you continuing to educate yourself outside of traditional schooling?

_____

_____

_____

_____

_____

_____

_____

2. In what ways might your own education have been taught from a biased perspective? Consider the books chosen for reading lists, the figures highlighted in textbooks, the languages offered, etc.

_____

_____

_____

_____

_____

_____

_____

_____

3. Do you think all countries should learn the same subjects? Why/why not?

Had you been born halfway across the world, would your current education be relevant?

_____

_____

_____

_____

_____

_____

_____

_____

_____

4. How much of your education was from formal education and how much was from life itself? Would you say you are more book smart or street smart? Which, in your current city, is more important to your overall success?

_____

_____

_____

_____

_____

_____

_____

_____

_____

5. In the columns, list the subjects you could spend all day studying and the subjects you tend to avoid.

I could spend all day studying...	I tend to avoid...

Why do you think you're interested in the topics you're interested in? What topics do others tend to seek your input on? What would you be knowledgeable enough to teach?

6. What is something you've discovered in life that you could have used more education on?

Which subjects were not available to you, but which you would have liked to study? Do you think your schooling was worth it, considering time and cost? How could it have been more efficient?

7. Imagine you're in school and your parents ask you to switch schools, whether across town or to another country, where you will be the new kid. What would you say to your parents?

Did you go to school with the same people your entire life? What effect did this have on your social life?

_____

_____

_____

_____

_____

_____

_____

_____

_____

8. It's your final year of school in your hometown. In general, where do people go next and what do they do? Is that what you did? Why/why not?

_____

_____

_____

_____

_____

_____

_____

_____

_____

9. List the topics that your family knows more about than the average family.

-
-
-
-
-

Are you interested in the same topics as your family? Is there a subject your family wanted you to learn more about, or a skill to pick up, that you didn't? How has your family's experience of education influenced you?

10. Based on your experiences in the world, in which ways are you smarter than other people? In which ways are others smarter than you?

Do you feel you're smarter on average than other people? Why do you think this is?

Nationality

I'VE NEVER felt more American than outside of the USA. It only takes one instance of bumping into a stranger on a subway abroad and immediately exclaiming "Oopsies" or casually giving out the temperature in Fahrenheit for me to fully realize that, as hard as I try to be my own version of a permanent expat, perennial backpacker, or vying candidate for the highest level of Global Citizenship, I may as well give into the fact that some things may never change: Maybe there are parts of me that will forever be branded a red, white, and blue-blooded American patriot for the rest of my life.

But I'm not surprised. Nearly the first label we learn to place on ourselves as children is one that refers back to nationality—needless to say, at age five we have no idea of the differences between being, say, Austrian and Australian; we have barely begun babbling our way through language, let alone learned to differentiate between what makes us *us* and them *them*. You see, before we can understand what it means to be Austrian or Australian, we need to see aspects that aren't representative of our nationality to fully grasp which aspects *are*. This is the case for five-year-olds first learning they have a nationality, just as it is for eighty-five-year-olds who are fully aware of their nationality but who have yet to explore beyond it.

We feel most like our nationalities outside our countries of origin because it's then when a bright spotlight shines upon a part of our identity we don't often get the chance to observe when surrounded by people with the same cultural frames of reference. This often happens abroad around the most insignificant, mundane activities back home. Daily grocery trips go from being a task to check off on the to-do list to a full-fledged cultural experiment: Half the ingredients of your daily diet aren't available, the produce is in kilos when you understand pounds, and you're trying to keep up small talk with the cashier, but they're already swiping the next customer's carrots. This is only the first stop, then you'll have all the miniscule differences at the post offices, restaurants, and bars, too. Although miniscule to some extent, these are the details that make you distinguishable from everyone else in the world.

Going abroad makes you feel more interest*ing* in that you're able to discover a "new" side of yourself—and by "new," I mean the same nationality that's been invisible to you this whole time. Additionally, you feel more interest*ed* toward life and toward continuing to put yourself in these foreign milieus to see what else might be revealed.

If we're always around people of the same nationality, we will always be around similar experiences, and as a result, we may have only very narrow reference point to explain how our life should look. The intention of this book is not to get you to disown your nationality but rather to acknowledge all the ways you are already representative of it, and to then imagine a reality in which everyone around the world acted as an independent agent, not basing our full identities on where we were born, but rather picking and choosing interesting aspects of each nationality and culture, and going from there. This isn't some far-off pipe dream; this is one that can and does happen today and it's called being a global citizen.

CHECK-IN

- Is your nationality one of the first adjectives you would use to describe yourself?

- What is a stereotype of your nationality and do you represent it?

- Who was the first person you met who was not your nationality?

- When was the last time you spent time with someone who was not your nationality?

- Is there a nationality that you're more curious about than others?

YOU ARE HERE

1. Imagine you're able to be reborn into another country of your choice and adopt a new nationality. Which would you choose? Why?

Do you already feel more like one nationality than another?

_____

_____

_____

_____

_____

_____

_____

_____

2. As a kid, what culture or country do you remember romanticizing?

Who or what drew you to this culture in the first place?

_____

_____

_____

_____

_____

_____

_____

_____

3. How much awareness do you have of the history of your country and how it was founded? If you were alive back in that time, would you have done things the same way?

_____

_____

_____

_____

_____

_____

_____

_____

4. Would you fly your country's flag over your home? Why or why not?

Is showing patriotism important in your culture? How have your country's recent history and politics influenced this? Does everyone know the lyrics to your country's national anthem? In school, did you have to salute your country's flag or recite a patriotic oath?

_____

_____

_____

_____

_____

_____

_____

_____

_____

5. In the columns, list a few countries with which your country has a certain affinity or negative rapport. Circle the column that, if you were to set off on your travels today, would excite you more.

+	−

6. You're abroad and hear a stranger criticizing your country. How would you respond to this criticism?

_____
_____
_____
_____
_____
_____
_____
_____
_____
_____
_____
_____
_____
_____
_____

7. What might others who don't live where you do not fully understand about life in your country?

What unique challenges does your country face? For example: the cost of living, government corruption, dwindling or aging population, imminent threat of war.

_____

_____

_____

_____

_____

_____

_____

_____

_____

8. Teachers in another country are teaching students about how to interact with someone from your nationality. What do you think they say about your nationality in terms of stereotypical personality traits, social codes, cultural values, and pastimes?

_____

_____

_____

_____

_____

_____

_____

_____

_____

9. What is a quality that most people of your nationality share that perhaps other nationalities could adopt?

_____

_____

_____

_____

_____

_____

_____

_____

_____

_____

10. Your country's government has sent you a letter requesting your help. They want you to be a secret agent abroad. Under what conditions would you accept or refuse that offer? Would this be the same answer if a foreign government asked you to spy on your home country's government?

_____

_____

_____

_____

_____

_____

_____

_____

_____

_____

Race and ethnicity

RACE IS OUR outermost layer and thus one of the first things a stranger notices about us. It sits there so silently and yet can say so much based on the cultures, behaviors, and norms we've attributed to it. Our race is based on the physical attributes we've inherited—skin color, hair color, hair texture, eye color, eye shape, etc.—while our ethnicity is rooted in our cultural ancestry. In other words, we can be of the same race but have different ethnicities, or have the same ethnicity but be of different races.

Skin color reflects thousands of years of our genetic lineage's proximity to the equator, according to which we, and therefore our skin, receive more or fewer hours of sunshine. We can see this reflected today in the countries nearest the equator having populations with darker skin tones, and those farthest away having lighter. This, paired with the same thousands of years of complicated historical relations consisting of land grabs, territorial invasions, and colonial conquests all contribute to our understandings, or perhaps rather, misunderstandings of other racial groups.

In the pursuit of becoming a global citizen, it's inevitable that, at one point or another, you will feel what it's like to be around people who look nothing like you—although maybe this is already a daily experience for you in your home country. For instance, perhaps you're enjoying your day in Marrakech, and find yourself confused when a random tourist asks for a photo with you—because they've never seen anyone like you in person. Perhaps, the vendor at the marketplace in Mumbai makes an assumption about your income on the color of your skin and charges you a higher or lower price. Perhaps the server in Chiang Mai is recommending a dish based on how spicy a level they think you can handle—and maybe they'll assume you do or do not know how to use chopsticks.

For someone reading a book like this, making outward acts of discrimination is not something they would ever do, but there may be other many minor, unforeseen biases that aren't directly racist by nature, but that point out how we do notice race itself, and not just abroad, but in our daily lives back home. Perhaps at a wedding, in a friendship group where everyone is Hispanic, you feel you need to tell everyone that the groom is a white guy; how you described someone as African American when they were Black but not American; how you have your preferences when it comes to hair salons that will understand your hair texture or therapists who you think, because they have a particular racial or ethnic background, will better understand what you've been through. Perhaps, you even hesitate when talking about race in the first place.

The conversation around race can be as complex as we'd like to make it, but it's one that concerns us all. A lack of exposure to other races will only expose your own deeply entrenched beliefs, as innocent as they may be. What's most important in stopping the cycle of perpetuating the same, tired stereotypes and assumptions from past generations is to make efforts to question our own biases and ignorance, whether black or white, so the conversation around race is not so black and white.

CHECK-IN

- Would you consider your race and ethnicity core parts of your identity?

- Do you feel more linked to your race or to your ethnicity? For example: do you feel more Irish than White, or more Black than English?

- Is the culture you're from mostly diverse or mostly homogenous?

- In your country, is race a hot topic?

- In your country, who tends to be in positions of power? For example, in government, presenting TV shows, teaching in a university?

YOU ARE HERE

1. How much of your life has been spent living and/or working among the majority or minority race of where you are from? Shade in the timeline of your life. Consider your first neighborhoods, schools, extracurricular activities, jobs, etc.

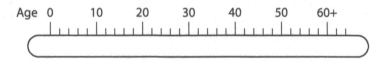

Age 0   10   20   30   40   50   60+

What impact has this had on you?

2. In what ways do you notice your race? Are you aware of your race on a daily basis?

_____

_____

_____

_____

_____

_____

_____

_____

_____

_____

_____

_____

_____

_____

_____

3. You're in rural Turkey and a local family wants you to wear their traditional outfit. Do you? It was the most fun you had in Turkey. Do you post it on social media?

What are your thoughts on society's perceptions of cultural appreciation and cultural appropriation? For example: you are Black, and appreciate Japanese culture. You are Middle Eastern, and appreciate Mexican culture. You are White, and appreciate Jamaican culture.

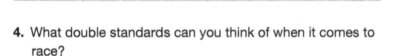

4. What double standards can you think of when it comes to race?

Is there still a reason for these to exist? Where do you see inconsistencies in your own beliefs?

5. Which clichés about your race do you find to be true?

When speaking about race with your closest friends and family, what is the vibe? Heavy and tense? Walking on eggshells? Light and jokey? Open to learning?

_____

_____

_____

_____

_____

_____

_____

_____

_____

_____

6. List out your friend group or people you have dated or been attracted to. What race were they?

Is it okay to have a preference when it comes to dating? Which race(s) are you objectively the least familiar with?

7. What are the most common immigration patterns to your city or country?

Which races are primarily represented in the town you spend the most time in?

_____

_____

_____

_____

_____

_____

_____

_____

_____

_____

8. If you were to adopt, would you feel comfortable raising a baby from abroad who doesn't look like you and whose culture you're unfamiliar with? Would you only want children if they have similar genetics?

_____

_____

_____

_____

_____

_____

_____

_____

_____

_____

9. The mayor's office of your local town has received a proposal to remove historical statues based on their problematic history around race and ethnicity. To what extent do you believe we should try to rectify the past?

10. In what ways might you currently be racist, whether you like to admit it or not? Be as honest as you can.

2
INTERNAL

WE SEE
THE
WORLD
NOT AS IT
IS, BUT AS
WE ARE.

—Anaïs Nin

PERHAPS YOU'VE experienced that moment when you turn the final page of a book, having been gripped from the start, and you excitedly tell your friend about how much you enjoyed the plot, only for them to stare quizzically back at you. You loved it. They hated it. What is on the page remains the same, but the way the page reads can vastly differ. These variations exist due to the content of our minds being completely and utterly unique to us at any given moment— made up of every lived experience, from every heartbreak we've endured to every milestone we've celebrated. It's why you burst into laughter at a dark joke, get emotional listening to country song lyrics, curse at the Jeep that cuts in front you on the highway, and why someone else would have an entirely different reaction. Multiply that by a lifetime of these experiences and you can see how we all experience the world with different internal makeups. So, it's not so much what happens in our world that's important, but how we react to it and the importance we attach to it.

In the "Internal" section, we explore this abstract side of life we can't quite put a finger on but which we collectively agree exists. We start by exploring the catalysts that sparked our **Passions and interests** and the extent to which we prioritize them in our lives. We then continue on to what it is that draws us to our **Friendships and connections** and the specific influences they've already had on us. The **Love and relationships** chapter explores our relationships to love, lust, and wanderlust. Next, we navigate our sometimes confusing and always flexible rapports within the spectrums of **Gender** and **Sexuality**. Finally, we end with the ways in which the rules around **Morals and taboos** differ from culture to culture, so that the definitions of good and bad are sometimes only relative.

As we move through our days and through our lives, it's important to remember that

ANYTHING THAT EVER HAPPENS AROUND YOU, TO YOU, OR FROM YOU IS AN OUTWARD REFLECTION OF SOMETHING THAT IS HAPPENING INTERNALLY.

It would be wise to get familiar with our relationship to these internal factors for while others only ever experience a part of us, we experience ourselves all day long.

We rarely know what's really going on with others, especially because we rarely know what's really going on with ourselves.

And now that we know this, let's try to change it.

Passions and interests

"WHAT DO you do when you're not working?" is my go-to, tried-and-true question when getting to know someone. By nature, it's a question that comes out of a workaholic American perpsective, as if work comes first and then everything else sneaks in after, but I've found it elicits more accurate responses about a person's life than the open-ended "What do you like to do?" whose unlimited possibilities feel a bit jarring, and honestly, not representative of how they actually spend their time, or, in other words, their life. "What do you do when you're not working?" asks the person to reflect on how they're really spending most of their free time. Is it on their hobbies or on their obligations?

Of course, there are many factors at play, and it's not as easy as dropping all obligations to pursue your passions; it's just that it's surprising that, in many societies around the world, we mostly accept the little free time we are given as just the way life is, saying things like "Well, how else is society supposed to work?" Observing life abroad would immediately show us that many countries offer a lot of vacation time, and we could demand the same in ours if only we were more aware of it. Equally, we might note the many digital nomads, remote workers, and people who have saved up and are traveling, and consider these are possibilities for us too. Instead, most of our free time often consists of just trying to keep up with life: responding to unread texts, cleaning the house, running errands, and distracting ourselves with an incessant stream of social media videos. Not that these aren't enjoyable, but it's only the few days, weeks, or months off we get for vacation—whichever is customary in the culture you work in—that we tend to have the energy to pursue our true passions and interests.

That said, traveling, and especially solo traveling, is a really good indicator of what activities you naturally gravitate toward. Why? Because you've finally got your time and mind freed up to consider them. Perhaps it's news to you that you actually don't care about checking out the latest exhibition at the top-rated museum; you'd rather lose yourself in the botanical garden, research the best vegan restaurants, or sweat it out at the beach volleyball courts.

It's not only when we're traveling that our location influences what we like to do; our interests are often influenced by where we grow up and where we call home. Cycling, for instance, is huge in the Netherlands, but which started first: the cycle lanes that inspired people to adopt the mode of transportation, or the demand for cycle lanes because people loved cycling? In either case, it is clear that the people of the Netherlands are cycling, and thus our culture has some influence in sparking our interests in hobbies in the first place. After all, it's not so easy to pick up a hobby like surfing in the US Midwest, just as it's likely not your first thought to learn about agriculture when you're living in south London.

These passions and interests that become our hobbies act as secret superpowers in daily life; no one can tell just by looking at us that we are conversationally fluent in Swahili, have extensively studied anthropology, or own a vintage postcard collection, and yet these are often the topics that light us up the most when we talk about them. To think that everyone around you, at any given moment, also possesses a unique set of passions and interests hidden to us at first glance is proof that the world around us is full of curious wonder. We never know what our future interests will be, nor the who, the what, or the where that will lead us to them.

It's only a matter of time.

CHECK-IN

- What hobbies are popular in your country or where you're from, and are they hobbies you are also interested in? For example: sports, cuisine, the arts.

- Are you aware of any hobbies that are popular abroad, but not in your country?

- Circle the word that applies to you: Based on my life thus far, it appears that I'm seeking a life of comfort/excitement. Is this the life you wanted?

- Does the lifestyle in your country tend to be more fast or slow paced?

- Do you feel you've already discovered your lifelong passion or do you feel like you are still discovering it as you go?

YOU ARE HERE

1. What do you do when you're not working?

Is the bulk of your time spent pursuing your passions and interests or spent more on obligations, killing time on social media, etc?

_____

_____

_____

_____

_____

_____

_____

2. In your culture, what activities do families tend to enroll their children in? For example: sports, music, dance, art, nature activities, religious education.

Did you do any of these and was this because of your own interest or your family's? Have you stuck with or grown out of these pastimes?

_____

_____

_____

_____

_____

_____

_____

3. Remember a time you were at peace. What can most take your mind off your studies, work, or other obligations?

_____

_____

_____

_____

_____

_____

_____

_____

_____

_____

4. If you won the lottery and never had to work again, what would you do differently with your time?

Does your current financial situation impact how you engage with your hobbies?

_____

_____

_____

_____

_____

_____

_____

_____

_____

_____

5. On a trip, which takes priority: what you want to do, or what everyone else wants to do?

In which ways do your interests conflict with or differ from those of your friends and family?

_____

_____

_____

_____

_____

_____

_____

_____

6. In which ways do you prioritize your passions? In which ways are you doing a disservice to your passions?

Are you always buying the cheapest running shoes even though you run every day? Are you setting aside money to invest in the stock market, but not on quality paint brushes you use daily? Are you spending too much time in front of a screen, when yet another one of those books you bought is left unread next to your bed?

_____

_____

_____

_____

_____

_____

_____

_____

7. Take a look at a world map. Where around the world best suits your passions, interests, or hobbies?

Would you consider moving to pursue your passions?

_____

_____

_____

_____

_____

_____

_____

_____

_____

_____

8. How do you think you would view your interests or hobbies if you were someone else who grew up in another country or culture?

_____

_____

_____

_____

_____

_____

_____

_____

_____

_____

9. What inspires/inspired your interests? Consider, for example, your role models, media, teachers, course subjects, extracurricular activities, and school sports.

_____

_____

_____

_____

_____

_____

_____

_____

_____

_____

_____

10. Pull up your calendar. When was the last time you truly felt alive? What activities were you doing at that moment?

_____

_____

_____

_____

_____

_____

_____

_____

_____

_____

_____

Friendships and connections

IT IS often said that we are the average of our five closest friends, but first, that assumes we have five friends, and second, I would add that we are more accurately the sum of a few distinct interactions here and there, and often ones made up of complete strangers and on-the-go friendships.

Everyone has a story similar to this one: you innocently sit down for brunch somewhere (in my case, Paris) when an eccentric older lady claiming she is psychic approaches the table and randomly blurting out, "You are an artist. Don't let anyone take advantage of you." Or perhaps you are playing tennis (in my case, in Indiana) when your French teacher's nonchalant whisper "You'll never know until you go" goes from being helpful advice to a motto that carries you from country to country throughout your twenties. These weren't life lessons I learned from being around my five closest friends, or five hundred closest friends for that matter; these were unexpected one-liners and free compliments that were effortlessly (and kindly) thrown my way, stuck with me over time, and inspired me to stay on track with what I really saw for my life. This isn't just me; you have these random interactions, too, and they've most likely shaped the person you've become and what you've done so far.

The very fleeting nature of travel will present us with many of these one-off scenarios and unspoken (or spoken) connections with people in passing—some of whom we'd love to stay around for longer. Indeed, there are interactions that last five seconds that can have a longer impression on us than those that last five years. Being a global citizen is about learning to live with these evanescent friendships that blossom within the four walls of a hostel, the row you were assigned on the train, or the gate at the airport. In fact, one of the greatest paradoxes of making global citizen friends in the first place is that, in order to discover the next group of fascinating people, we must detach ourselves from the last. Whether it was Vitor in São Paulo, Felix in Montréal, or Jack in Dublin, I knew we would be good friends if only we lived in the same city, and yet in order to meet Vitor in São Paulo, Félix in Montréal, or Jack in Dublin, I had to leave each one of them to get to meet the next one.

While friendships clearly have a (mainly) positive effect on a person, the most important friendship we can have is with ourselves, especially if we are to have good relationships with others. Case in point: One night in Paris, my wanderlust took me to a club, aptly named *Wanderlust*, where after spotting a handsome man across the dance floor, an irritating (yet thought-provoking) French "friend" had me wondering about my own lust. I asked my friend if we should go talk to this beautiful *inconnu*, to which he quickly snapped, "Why are you so desperate for social interaction? Aren't you good enough here with just me?" I almost spat out my sauvignon. But isn't part of going out letting yourself go all out? According to my American upbringing, in order to have the best time, everyone needed to know they were always welcome to join in.

Nonetheless, I disregarded his comment and shocked my friend further by waving the guy over. A few boring conversations later, I shook my head as I witnessed my friend exit the club with the same guy he had scolded me for inviting over in the first place. His words "But why are you so desperate for social interaction? Aren't you good enough here with just me?" echoed in my head.

I stood alone with my sauvignon. Although my glass looked half-empty to some, my glass was half-full to me. This was a moment I had been confronted with solo trip after solo trip: How can anyone enjoy your company if you can't enjoy your own? I raised my glass to *Wanderlust* and caught my reflection in the middle of the dance floor: Damon D, you've got a friend in me.

CHECK-IN

- Are you the same person with others as you are alone? What about with different people?

- How often do you do things publicly, alone? For example: eating at restaurants, going to the movies.

- What sentences or advice have stuck with you over time?

- In what context(s) have you made the majority of your friends? For example: at school, in work, on trips, in bars, online.

- Who is someone you are not close to, but has still had an impact on you today?

YOU ARE HERE

1. Name your closest friends throughout your life:

Note down their age, race, nationality, sexuality, gender, profession, astrological sign, where you met, how many years you've known them. What patterns do you notice and why are you drawn to these people?

2. Draw a zigzag to represent mountains. Place the friends who make you feel the best along the peaks and the others along the valleys.

3. Consider the last falling-out you had with a friend. Now that time has passed, how do you feel about this? Has your reaction to this changed?

How does verbal confrontation make you feel? Do you shy away from it, even if you think you're in the right, because you fear the loss of the friendship? Or do you stand up for what you believe to be true, even if this risks the friendship? Do people from your culture typically tend to shy away from confrontation or fully take it on? How easy is it for you to forgive?

_____

_____

_____

_____

_____

_____

_____

4. One of your closest friends just informed you that they're moving halfway across the world. Write down your text message to them:

_____

_____

_____

_____

_____

_____

_____

_____

Do you adopt a congratulatory tone? Do you hide your disappointment? Do you beg them to stay? Or do you secretly resent them?

5. You're invited to a house party, but no one you know has arrived yet. Are you more of the type to approach others or wait to be approached?

What is your level of openness to strangers? How quickly are you willing to expand your social circle? Would you say you're from a warm and friendly culture, or one that's more distant and respectful?

_____

_____

_____

_____

_____

_____

_____

_____

6. Who, thus far in your life, has had the greatest impact on you? What percentage of your current self would you attribute to them?

_____

_____

_____

_____

_____

_____

_____

_____

_____

7. Would you consider yourself to be more comfortable with formality or informality? Is your culture generally more formal or informal with others?

_____

_____

_____

_____

_____

_____

_____

_____

_____

_____

8. How would you react if all of your current friendship group moved away? Would you be more likely to also move, or instead stay put and make new friends?

How much of where you call home is influenced by the friendships and connections in your life? Do you have any close friends who live far away?

_____

_____

_____

_____

_____

_____

_____

_____

_____

_____

9. Describe your hardest goodbye.

Why was it so hard? Who was it with?

_____

_____

_____

_____

_____

_____

_____

_____

_____

_____

_____

10. Would you be friends with yourself if you met yourself?

Why do other people keep you around? Why might someone not want to be your friend?

_____

_____

_____

_____

_____

_____

_____

_____

_____

_____

_____

_____

Love and relationships

L **IS** for the way you look at ... yourself.

Some psychologists argue that you fall in love with people not because you love *them*, but because of how they make *you* feel about *yourself*. As your intimacy heightens, fewer boundaries exist, making you feel more comfortable to show off more vulnerable sides of yourself that you might not have shown at first. Through this process, you feel more and more understood, accepted, and validated by someone for even the rawest sides of yourself, and thus, you wish to keep them around because now you, too, realize your rawest sides maybe aren't so terrible after all if someone else seems fine with them. Fittingly, *you* become attached, not necessarily because of something they're doing on their end, but because of your own internal processes. So, the next time someone tells you, "It's not you, it's me," they could actually be telling you the truth.

French writer Marcel Proust said:

IT IS OUR IMAGINATION THAT IS RESPONSIBLE FOR LOVE, NOT THE OTHER PERSON.

And I can surely attest to that, Monsieur Proust. Time and time again, I find myself on a train or plane wondering why it always seems not only more magical, but so much easier to fall in love while on a trip. Cue to table four at Café Slavia in Prague, where I sat opposite my date: a blond-haired, blue-eyed British expat with a rugby player build and a vocabulary that included words like "cheeky" and "ghastly." He ordered his schnitzel in fluent Czech with a slightly posh English accent and teased me for my quirks, like writing the day and month "backwards" (according to him), or opening the window to improve the lack of airflow in the restaurant. Although I immediately became hyper aware of my Americanness, it was this same Americanness that made me instantly feel like the profile I had to offer was an interesting one—and being in the Czech Republic at the time, a unique one. This hypothesis must have been somewhat valid, for what began as a three-hour date evolved into a three-day love-athon consisting of people-watching in the Old Town, slipping into abandoned Baroque ballrooms, and picnicking along the Vltava River.

To add to the thrill, it was all unfurling in what I refer to as the infamous last-day curse, where you discover something or someone interesting only at the last moment when it's nearly too late. Although I had been in Prague for nearly two weeks, it was only during my final days that we met. But perhaps it's worth considering another perspective: that the last-day curse be seen as a blessing in disguise since it's the knowledge that these international relationships can last only a few brief hours that allows us to revel in and live out every moment like it's our last. Because with them, it literally could be. In other words, it's this very idea that attracts us and creates a dynamic spark in the first place.

Whether we're traveling or falling in love, at the end of the day, what it seems we're really looking for is a reminder that we're alive.

Imagine doing them both at the same time.

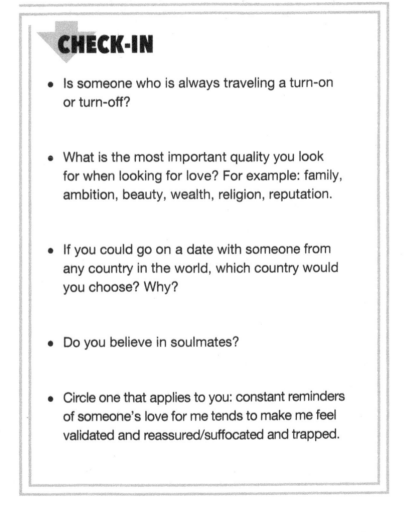

CHECK-IN

- Is someone who is always traveling a turn-on or turn-off?

- What is the most important quality you look for when looking for love? For example: family, ambition, beauty, wealth, religion, reputation.

- If you could go on a date with someone from any country in the world, which country would you choose? Why?

- Do you believe in soulmates?

- Circle one that applies to you: constant reminders of someone's love for me tends to make me feel validated and reassured/suffocated and trapped.

YOU ARE HERE

1. List all of the people you've ever dated in your life:

Circle those who aren't from the same culture as you. Highlight those that were a different race from you. Underline those who were from a different region or country. Star those who speak a different native language. Jot down where you met each. Do you recognize any patterns?

2. From a partner's perspective, what are your strengths and weaknesses in a relationship? Complete the chart:

Strengths	Weaknesses

Are any of these qualities representative of the culture you grew up in?

3. You're exchanging intense eye contact with someone on the train and believe it's love at first sight. This person gets off the train at the next stop. Do you get off to say something? Why or why not?

_____

_____

_____

_____

_____

_____

_____

_____

_____

4. What are your views on monogamy, serial-monogamy or having multiple partners?

How have your culture's views on relationships, dating, marriage, monogamy and polygamy influenced your own thoughts about it?

_____

_____

_____

_____

_____

_____

_____

_____

_____

5. You're going through a rough patch in your relationship
when someone who's just your type offers to buy you a
drink. What would you do?

Where do you draw the line between flirting and cheating?
Does infidelity tend to be a deal breaker in your culture?

---

6. Is there an archetype for the perfect partner in your
culture?

---

7. How does your culture regard forgiveness? Is it acceptable or common to remain civil with past partners?

_____

_____

_____

_____

_____

_____

_____

_____

_____

_____

8. Your trip abroad is coming to a close, but you feel you've found the love of your life. Would you overstay a visa for love?

How much of your current lifestyle are you willing to sacrifice for love?

_____

_____

_____

_____

_____

_____

_____

_____

_____

_____

9. In the case of an arranged marriage, who would your family choose for you to be with, based on their preferences? Would you be ok with this choice of person?

_____
_____
_____
_____
_____
_____
_____
_____
_____

10. Would you be OK with spending the majority of your life single?

Would your culture accept those who spend their life single as much as it would those who spend their life in a relationship?

_____
_____
_____
_____
_____
_____
_____
_____
_____
_____

Gender

WHETHER WE are a student in Pennsylvania, a waiter in New York, a nurse in London, a Brazilian expat in Indonesia, a South African diplomat, or a World Cultures major, the first thing that people often notice about us is our gender expression. Whether we align closely with the masculine or feminine, or fall somewhere in between, understanding that gender is a social construct and varies depending on the culture you are in is an important concept.

At this point we're no stranger to placing the rigid binary labels male or female on ourselves to make others (and ourselves) feel comfortable. Within seconds of our birth, we're traditionally greeted with a blue or pink balloon and celebrated for our sex. Everyone will ask, "Is it a boy or girl?" and in our minds, all of the imagined life paths unfold in seconds. Boys will gravitate toward cars and toy dinosaurs and girls will play with dolls and makeup, because we will only give them these things and tell them they like them. Years will go by and we'll casually throw around expressions like "Boys will be boys" as a blanket excuse for boys displaying unsavory behavior, but for the same behavior, we'll tell girls they are "too emotional" or that they are being "too much of a girl."

Our society has cemented these gender roles for so long that we subconsciously take part in this too, with our daily language subtly reinforcing the idea that femininity is inferior. It is common practice for men to use Mr., but for women to not only differentiate between Miss, Ms., and Mrs., but also take on the male partner's last name at marriage. Additionally, nearly all of our language in English used to make someone appear weak and undesirable are derived from the feminine: "You hit like a girl!"

We're not just undermining the value of feminine qualities; we're making it so that men feel they have to behave in a certain way too. We would poke fun at a masculine man who is jamming out to a female pop star and we might be taken aback by men crying in public ("Boys don't cry! Man up!"). Then we wonder why most people who commit crimes are men, whose pent-up emotions likely manifest as anger and violence. Gender has always been a flexible concept and yet we so often shame each other into internalizing and abiding by a binary that none of us should have to follow in the first place.

Where before a lot of the world only operated in this binary—you're male or female and all other deviation is unacceptable—many cultures are just now opening up to the idea that we've been living on vast gender and sexuality spectrums and only occupying so little of them, as if it's a matter of a strict game of tug-of-war where we can only choose one side. The game of tug-of-war still works for many, but for others, they either want to be in the middle of that rope or nowhere near it.

In a world where we've accepted that there are different ways to approach life—spiritual practices, political views, cultural values, etc.—it's surprising to me that rigid attitudes toward gender and sexuality remain consistent—and yet, we can see from cultures all around the world that deviating from the binary construct of male versus female isn't an unprecedented phenomenon or one that is even unique to one part of the world; it's a reoccurring one, from the kathoey identity in Thailand to hijra identity in India. Gender-variant people have been documented time and time again, and around the world at that—and these are just a few of the groups that have been recorded in recent history.

In this pursuit of becoming global citizens, we have to continuously remind ourselves where our current thought processes stem from. The ideology that exists today is based on patterns of colonization, and the influence of its cultural preferences thereafter. If another part of the world where this gender fluidity was integrated had risen to hegemonic power, we would have most likely adopted their way. It's really a question of the same game of tug-of-war, but just who got to the rope first.

It's understandable that many feel their identity has already been defined and, at this point, may feel uncomfortable about experimenting with different gender identities. After all, for most people alive today, our identities have been built atop a gender pattern we've had ingrained in us from our first seconds of life. We've mostly accepted the qualities that we were told fit nicely into our gender identity and denied ourselves to others. But whether our own relationship to gender has been explored or not, what's important to note is that it's a topic that concerns us all. Why for example, do companies gender non-gendered products like socks or razors for monetary gain? Why as a society do we expect women to shave body hair but men not to? In challenging gender norms as a whole, we too will benefit from a new, more flexible freedom of expression. The options are limitless, and always have been.

- Shade in the percentage of how masculine or feminine, or neither, you feel.

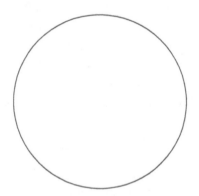

- If you had the option to choose the gender of your future child, would you have a preference? And would you be open to them having a different gender identity?

- How much does someone's gender expression (i.e., how someone presents themselves) affect you, whether positively or negatively?

- Are you from a culture that is more matriarchal or more patriarchal? When growing up, which family figure was mostly in charge?

- Circle one that applies to you: Compared to those around me, I am more/less attached to gender than they are.

YOU ARE HERE

1. What are your views on people changing their names when they marry? Would you expect or be expected to change your name?

Which last names in your family history are you currently aware of? Were these from your mom's or dad's side? Would you be prepared to change your name if you married?

_____

_____

_____

_____

_____

_____

_____

_____

_____

2. Your child is curious about the world. To what extent do you allow them to explore notions of masculinity and femininity and to what extent do you try influencing them in a direction? In what ways were you influenced by your parents?

_____

_____

_____

_____

_____

_____

_____

_____

3. In which ways might you benefit from societal gender norms? For example: being able to walk home safely at night because you are a man; getting maternity leave or child custody because you are a woman.

_____

_____

_____

_____

_____

_____

_____

_____

_____

_____

4. How do gender norms today differ from those of your parents' generation (if at all)? How do they view this change or lack thereof? Are you from a culture that is willing to adopt new ideas, or one that preserves tradition as much as possible?

_____

_____

_____

_____

_____

_____

_____

_____

_____

_____

5. What stereotypes do you still think accurately apply to another gender, even though these may still be controversial?

Do you view men or women of other nationalities differently to how you view men or women with the same nationality as you?

_____

_____

_____

_____

_____

_____

_____

_____

_____

_____

6. Off the top of your head, list five topics you think another gender spends a lot of their time speaking about. Do you personally know anyone for whom this is accurate?

-

-

-

-

-

7. You have to spend the rest of the month traveling with people of another gender. In which ways would this be easy or difficult for you?

_____

_____

_____

_____

_____

_____

_____

_____

_____

_____

8. Do you have any gender preferences when it comes to certain professions? Consider a scenario in which you needed to hire a therapist, doctor, teacher, private investigator, nanny, construction worker and so on. Why do you prefer who you prefer?

_____

_____

_____

_____

_____

_____

_____

_____

_____

_____

9. What inconsistencies or double standards can you think of in terms of gender within your culture? For example: women have to wear a traditional uniform, but men do not; women might hug at a meeting, but men shake hands. Do you find these make sense?

_____

_____

_____

_____

_____

_____

_____

_____

10. In which ways do you feel attached to your gender?

Is there something that you hold back doing because it's associated with another gender, or do you regularly challenge gender norms? For example: having a man as a bridesmaid, playing extreme sports, wearing a tight pink T-shirt, shaving body hair, crying in public, raising your voice, etc.

_____

_____

_____

_____

_____

_____

_____

_____

Sexuality

A FEW years ago, while volunteering at a hostel in Lisbon, I noticed that in addition to the daily walking tour or nightly bar crawl, what most guests were looking for, whether German, Canadian, Brazilian, or Australian (you can be sure there'll always be at least one), was to meet someone they vibed with. Some did.

I did.

My attraction to Bruna surprised me because she was not a man. She was tan, brunette, and charming in the sense that she'd ask where you're from and then use her insider cultural knowledge from working the front desk of an international hostel to tease you about it all night. I think everyone was in love with her, actually. After a communal hostel dinner, we ventured out to a club under a bridge (typical for Europe), where all the hostel guests vied for her attention as if they were contestants on an episode of *The Bachelorette*. I may have lost her that night, but I've never lost hope since.

It was not so long ago that I was convinced I wasn't attracted to anyone; then convinced I wasn't attracted to the same sex; then later convinced I wasn't attracted to the opposite sex. Now I am convinced I should no longer be convinced about anything. This sexuality rollercoaster leads me to my sneaking suspicion that much of human sexuality is more fluid than the label we assign people; it's just that we either haven't found the person who gives us that electrical spark, or have, but haven't been open to the attraction due to our subconscious barriers or because we fear the consequences of defying our culture's expectations of sexuality.

In fact, if we examine labels like gay or straight, we realize it's not just because we're gay or straight that we are automatically attracted to everyone else who is also gay or straight. Attraction, even within our sexuality labels, always comes down to the specific person. To worry about a label at this point seems obsolete and irrelevant. But speaking of "straight" men...

There once was a Russian server at an event who spilled white wine on me. I said it was fine because 1) I wanted to practice my recent interest in Russian anyway and 2) he was fine, too. His frantic attempt to help me clean up was cute, not to mention I was possibly more in love with the idea of a meet cute than the love itself that comes of it. We exchanged numbers, and a few days later I was ecstatic when, in the middle of a London dance floor at 4 a.m., I received the notification "Dinner Monday? We go to Russian restaurant." I accepted, all in the name of culture, of course.

One hour before our "date," he asked if his girlfriend could join us. If you know anything about Russian cuisine, you would know that I was definitely not attending this dinner "date" for the vegetarian *golubtsi* on my plate. *Privyet!* (Hello!) I believed I was privy to a side of him that others weren't. See, being anything other than heterosexual in a majority ... heterosexual world is both thrilling and ... often disappointing in that you can never be quite sure who is interested and who isn't, and also because sometimes the people you're interacting with themselves don't know either. Throw in unknown cultural context clues, ambiguous texts, and incorrect copy and pastes from Google Translate, and you need an advanced degree in psycho-linguistic multimodal communication to be sure you're both actually flirting. Turns out, we weren't.

- Shade in the pie chart to describe your sexuality (e.g. 20% straight, 80% gay).

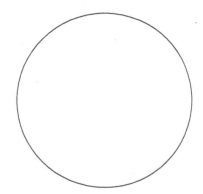

- Who is someone from a gender you're not typically attracted to that you find to be a good catch?

- Is your culture more or less tolerant of various sexualities than others?

- Someone's telling you about how many partners they've had. After what number would you raise your eyebrows?

- In your culture, how are children told where babies came from?

YOU ARE HERE

1. List a few of your sexual partners.

Note down their age, race, nationality, sexuality, gender, profession, astrological sign, how long you've known them, and where you met them. What patterns do you notice and why were you drawn to these people?

2. List the qualities you find attractive in a partner. Then categorize these traits as masculine or feminine:

masculine   feminine

Where might these have come from? Do you feel like your taste and desires are set or still evolving?

3. What is a personality trait you find attractive that doesn't seem to excite anyone else as much?

For example: You find your partner's fiery passion about politics admirable. You find someone's nerdiness cute.

4. Who was your first childhood crush?

Would you still have a crush on them today? Do you notice any patterns in regard to your sexuality today? When did you first become aware of your sexuality? How has your sexuality changed over time? To what extent, and how, would you say your culture has impacted your sexuality?

5. Your child is going through puberty. Do you teach them about sex or let them discover it on their own?

How did you learn about sex? How strict would you be as a parent regarding this topic? How is sex ed taught in your country? Are aspects of sex and sexuality still a rather taboo topic?

_____

_____

_____

_____

_____

_____

_____

_____

_____

6. It's the morning after and you're leaving the apartment of someone you just slept with. What do the next few hours look like? Would you feel judged by your culture for a one-night stand? For any sexual experience?

_____

_____

_____

_____

_____

_____

_____

_____

_____

7. Can you separate love and sex?

Have you ever had sex without being in love? Equally, have you ever been in love but didn't have sex?

8. Do you have any personal hang-ups about sex?

Do you feel any shame around the act of sex? Do you always need to have the lights on or off? Do you need to be drunk? Does being naked feel bizarre? Where are your boundaries? Have you accepted them as they are, or do you actively try to overcome them?

9. You've been dating someone for a few years and their appearance drastically changes to a look that you don't find attractive. To what extent does your attraction toward them change?

_____

_____

_____

_____

_____

_____

_____

_____

_____

_____

10. Someone mistakenly thinks you are gay/straight/bisexual. Write down your verbal reaction: Is it different from your inner reaction?

_____

_____

_____

_____

_____

_____

_____

_____

_____

_____

Morals and taboos

WHY DOES bad feel so good? Is it perhaps because you don't consider what's bad that bad after all, but you're living within a context that tells you it is? Perhaps it's the sense of rebellion that makes you feel alive, and thus it's the bad that makes you feel so good? Or perhaps it's the bad that makes you feel bad, and you'd be better off halfway across the world where your rebellion isn't rebellion at all?

What I find most interesting about what's morally right and wrong is that we mostly accept what's taught to us as given, and as the way society should be: that marriage be exclusively between two people, that we do not defy authority, that we do not consume psychedelic drugs, and so on and so forth. We often mindlessly give away our right to judge what's right and what's wrong to someone else who, like us, had free rein to question the status quo and decide for themselves what is right and wrong, but instead, we mostly adopt, abide by, and build our moral framework upon theirs. Is it that we truly believe that marriage should be exclusively between two people, that we should not defy authority, or that we should not consume any drugs? Or is it that we have simply been influenced enough to agree that's the way it always should have been and always should be?

Luckily for us, some have been rebellious enough to deviate from the rigid rules governments and religions have defined as the correct "moral code," hence the progress we've seen in our lifetimes (at least in some countries): the societal narrative shifting from one of discrimination to one of greater inclusion of many races, religions, genders, and sexual identities. While the law will always be an ever-changing pendulum swinging from political party to political party, by way of each and every nip, tuck, and tighten to the law, each generation is growing up with a new point of moral reference built upon the last. We can see this with each new generation being more accepting of things previous generations saw as morally wrong.

In the same way that people of different generations are currently walking around with varying degrees of morality, the same can also be said for people of different nationalities. We're taught what's good and bad not only in the context of the time we're alive, but by a cultural viewpoint that is already encouraging certain values. The focus may be on the individual or the community, the religion or lack thereof, or the adaptation to modernity or preservation of the country's traditions. As a result of others reacting to our behavior, we learn to emphasize the sides of us that are going to be accepted and suppress those that aren't. In other words, the notions of good and bad behavior are molded around our culture's already-existing interpretation of these definitions— and the extent to which we internalize or deconstruct these definitions is ultimately up to us and how much we're aware of other cultures' definitions of the same rules.

While most cultures seem to have signed off on a universal agreement of basic manners: holding a door for someone, giving up one's seat on public transportation for the elderly, or not disclosing darker moments from someone's past in public, there are other moral judgments, practices, and beliefs that have been twisted and turned upside down: showing skin in Brazil is nothing to get alarmed about, but showing skin in the Midwestern USA is. Drinking a daily glass of wine in France is a forgivable admission at the doctor's office, but doing so in the parts of the Middle East would be outing your lack of discipline. Buying magic psilocybin truffles in a coffee shop in Amsterdam is taxed and regulated, but would carry a criminal charge in Arkansas, let alone most of the world.

All of this to say: Travel and you'll discover that what you thought was your greatest vice is, to many, not a vice at all. Whether you think what you're doing is right or wrong, according to some culture somewhere, you're probably right.

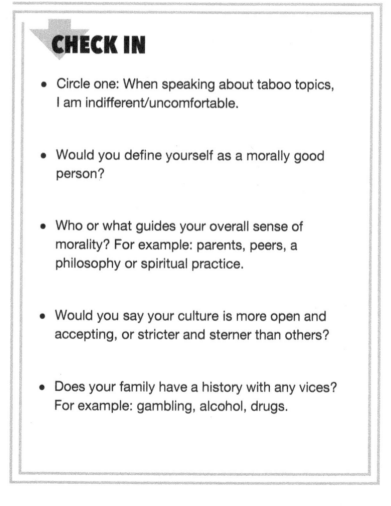

CHECK IN

- Circle one: When speaking about taboo topics, I am indifferent/uncomfortable.

- Would you define yourself as a morally good person?

- Who or what guides your overall sense of morality? For example: parents, peers, a philosophy or spiritual practice.

- Would you say your culture is more open and accepting, or stricter and sterner than others?

- Does your family have a history with any vices? For example: gambling, alcohol, drugs.

YOU ARE HERE

1. What do you find taboo? What is taboo elsewhere that you don't find taboo at all?

_____

_____

_____

_____

_____

_____

_____

_____

2. A friend's laptop is broken and they need to borrow yours for the day. Do you delete your search history before you give it to them?

What is in your search history that you're afraid of others' seeing? Is it that you really find it morally wrong in and of itself, or more that you are afraid of others' opinion of you changing?

_____

_____

_____

_____

_____

_____

_____

_____

3. It's 11:59 p.m. What is keeping you up at night? For example: money, safety, appearance, school, work, etc.

Are these based on your culture's expectations of what it means to be a good citizen? Would moving to a new culture solve any of these?

_____

_____

_____

_____

_____

_____

_____

_____

_____

4. What is an unpopular opinion you hold that even your closest friends would disagree with?

_____

_____

_____

_____

_____

_____

_____

_____

_____

_____

_____

5. To what extent is it culturally permitted to critique or confront your friends' points of view?

6. Write a list in which you confess your addictions. For example: the things in your life that have a strong grip over you, from a morning coffee to binge-watching a television series to having one too many drinks.

Who in your life can you open up to about anything and everything, as controversial as it may be?

7. In your country, are those in authority positions (politicians, police officers, owners of corporations etc.) generally to be trusted, or thought to be corrupt?

In the event of an emergency, would you get the police involved or avoid this?

---

8. You've found a wallet on the subway with no ID, but $500 in cash. What do you do?

Do you believe the average person in your country could be trusted to turn it in? Do you believe the average person from another country could be trusted to do so? Why do you think this?

---

9. How much have you been exposed to in terms of nudity, profanity, and violence, and how has this impacted you? Think about the shows you watch, the environment you grew up in, etc.

Is it important to be sheltered to some extent or given free rein to express oneself? Where do you stand on censorship?

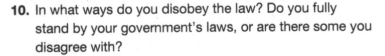

10. In what ways do you disobey the law? Do you fully stand by your government's laws, or are there some you disagree with?

What laws would you naturally be breaking if you were in another country? What is something you've done that's questionable? Do you feel guilty, indifferent, or proud of it? Would you say you're a rebellious person?

3
EXTERNAL

GIVE
AWAY
CONTROL
AND YOU
WILL
FINALLY
HAVE IT.

—*Alan Watts*

IT WASN'T until I was 30 that I realized I had been going through my life teetering between two seemingly incompatible schools of thought: that we are absolutely the ones in control of our life trajectory, and contrastingly, that we are absolutely not.

Why does it feel that some of the happenings in our life were meant to be—all the interesting people we've encountered, all the odd synchronicities, and all the timely "being in the right place at the right times" that propelled us to the next step of our lives—while others seem not to be caused by fate or some higher world order but are rather the result of our own decisions and efforts?

COULD IT SIMPLY BE THAT SOME EVENTS ARE PREDESTINED, AND SOME AREN'T?

Is there some greater string pulling by the universe that guides us along the path of our lives, or is that a whole lot of nonsense that we use to soothe ourselves because, deep-down, we can't handle the bleak existential truth that there's nothing greater out there and thus no real meaning to any of reality? Nonetheless, in either case, there always appear to be external forces beyond our control at play: the political party that gets elected to government, an unexpected pregnancy, a tragic bankruptcy, a sudden career change, or even a surprise discovery of the love of your life. This final "External" section revolves around the events in our lives that seem to happen to us, no matter how much peace we've made with our origins or how strong a grasp we have on our internal world.

In the following chapters, we're looking outward toward all that exists outside of us: the **Politics** category dives into how, for society to function as it does, we are subject to contributing to governments we may or may not have voted for, which then influence how our life plays out. In **Internet and media**, we look at how technology and the internet has helped introduce and connect us to the rest of the world. We'll explore how our nation's currency and relationships to money influence our own relationship with it in **Money and career**. We then dive into how our self-esteem and self-image are often based on others' opinions about us in relation to our culture's **Beauty and body** standards. Next, we'll examine the cultural traditions around **Food and drink** such as how mealtimes and table manners differ across the world. Finally, we'll wrap up the book with one of the most obviously influential external factors of all: **Travel and the world**.

We may never know if we are the driving force behind our lives or if it's down to some higher power, but there is one thing we do know: We're here in it now. It's time to take our relationship with reality and the external world and make it even more real.

Politics

FROM THE get-go, we are immediately exposed and subjected to the political leanings of the six o'clock news of our hometowns, one-off remarks from our close-knit and well-intentioned families, and the seemingly innocent small talk about the latest election with our fellow locals, all of which contribute to our innermost framework and influence our understandings of how the world works. But it would be a mistake to take these conclusions of the world based on our place in it and apply them to others' regions where people might have entirely different political leanings, six o'clock news programs, family relationships, and seemingly innocent small-talk, and yet, unfortunately, that's often exactly what happens.

As a joke for my YouTube channel, and out of genuine curiosity, I took a flight from Paris, France, to Paris, Texas. For a namesake, could there be a starker difference in terms of culture, cuisine, politics, and thus ... people? After the obligatory selfie with the replica Eiffel Tower—the one with a red cowboy hat tipped to the side—I pulled into the only highway diner around for miles, where I immediately noticed how segregated the diner was, except for the two things they all had in common: the gun on their holsters, and the diner-wide disapproval of the television's latest headline: "Government Proposes Nationwide Minimum Wage Hike." The word in Paris, Texas, was that this increase in wages might be nice temporarily, but would ultimately lead to a chain of events that included workers losing their jobs because employers could no longer afford them and more expensive omelets they themselves could no longer afford.

As I stared at my $3.50 bowl of oatmeal, it dawned on me that I had literally traveled from one extreme of the political spectrum to the other, where the only thing that remained constant was the impatience to see beyond one's own political context. In fact, when traveling, it becomes clearer that much of political beef is so often a misunderstanding of context. We don't just support what we support out of the blue; we each have a supporting rationale based on our own experience—an experience rooted in its own context that others will have never lived and, oftentimes, will not have ever been aware of. For instance, perhaps in your context it's obvious that the police show up when you call in an emergency or that the potholes in the street quickly get filled in as soon as they're noticed, but halfway across the world, or in the next town over for that matter, the police can't be relied upon in an emergency and you're just going to have to learn to swerve around the potholes. To apply blanket statements to other contexts is to not fully be aware of one's own context in the first place.

As much as some of us don't want to take part in the often-heated conversation around politics, it's important to realize that politics has contributed to who you are today. Depending on where you're from, your education, your healthcare, and your city infrastructure were all once a series of proposed programs and plans that were then funded by the tax contributions of the generations before you. Our country's rapport with politics goes a lot farther than just policy; it seeps into our understanding of how external society works. It's why Brazilians have the expression "jeitinho brasileiro" when they find a creative way around the rules, and why a Romanian friend of mine wasn't surprised when there weren't escalators at the central train station ... and why I was. She didn't expect her government to provide them, because she didn't expect much from her government anyway, whereas it was the first thing I noticed as I hauled my overweight suitcase up stair after stair. "Why hasn't someone fixed this?" I wondered, thinking of how, if the USA does one thing correctly, it's comfort and convenience. Because I was applying my relationship with politics to a context where it didn't apply.

Fortunately, traveling places you within these various political contexts. In other words, you're placed in a real life where, because you briefly experience it first-hand, you then get more of an accurate idea of why someone would have any motive for supporting their view. In this way, travel humanizes your political discourse; you're able to see outside your own fishbowl and how perhaps even your own previously firmly held political beliefs were a misunderstanding on your part. When you start seeing people, and not politics, the dense barriers between us quickly start fading away.

Lastly, in the same way you can exist independently without clinging to one political party's ideology, you can also exist independently without clinging to one country's ideology. There is an entire world out there of free spirits and freethinkers, unconcerned with hard-

and-fast agendas and nationalistic indoctrination. Those who have the most political insight are often the ones who have learned how the rest of the world works. Those people are global citizens.

CHECK-IN

- Name the political topic that gets you the most passionate:

- Growing up, most people around me were _____ (political party). Today, most people around me are _____ (political party).

- Circle the word that best applies to you: compared to other countries around the world, my country tends to skew more conservative/ liberal.

- How politically aware or engaged are you?

- What person or event sparked an interest in politics for you?

YOU ARE HERE

1. How do the elderly and the youth typically view the past, present and future of your country? For example: positively, negatively, hopefully, despondently, etc. Fill in the table.

How has the international perception of your country changed over time?

	Past	Present	Future
Elderly			
Youth			

2. You're the newly elected leader of your country. What is your first order of business and why?

Is there a country where your point of view on this topic is the preferred one and has already been implemented?

_____

_____

_____

_____

_____

_____

_____

_____

3. On which topics have your political views changed over time?

What events in your life might have caused them to change?

_____

_____

_____

_____

_____

_____

_____

_____

_____

_____

4. Do you feel that having strong borders is necessary or should we, as humans, be able to roam freely?

How would you improve your country's borders and immigration policy? If your country were in political turmoil, would you want to stay or leave for another country? What if the emigration process was extremely difficult and emigrating could take years?

_____

_____

_____

_____

_____

_____

_____

_____

_____

5. Someone at dinner is talking about a political issue you know a lot about. Describe your reaction, both internal and external:

Is your reaction different depending on who is speaking? Is your reaction different depending on whether you agree or disagree with them?

_____

_____

_____

_____

_____

_____

_____

_____

_____

_____

6. Consider your position on a few political issues. Now analyze the opposing viewpoint. In what ways is the rationale for such opinions understandable?

_____

_____

_____

_____

_____

_____

_____

_____

_____

_____

7. The latest news headline has you heated and you want your government to know how unhappy you are. To what extent can you protest or speak out freely against your government and its representatives (policymakers, police officers, judges, etc.)?

_____

_____

_____

_____

_____

_____

_____

_____

_____

_____

8. It's a tight election between two candidates no one particularly cares for. Your friends say they will vote for a third party that most likely won't win, but whose politics they actually support. What do you say?

_____

_____

_____

_____

_____

_____

_____

_____

_____

_____

9. You're starting to date someone and realize you have opposing political ideologies. How important is this detail in the future of your relationship?

Are you able to get along in other ways, or is this difference too large to be overlooked?

_____

_____

_____

_____

_____

_____

_____

_____

_____

_____

10. In what nonpolitical ways could you still get along with people on the opposite side of the political spectrum to you?

_____

_____

_____

_____

_____

_____

_____

_____

_____

Internet and media

BACK WHEN chatting online with complete strangers was a novel idea, I befriended a girl named Carmen from Beverly Hills. She would recount her nights spent sneaking out with socialite friends, driving her mom's red convertible through the Hollywood Hills, and then crawling back in through the window before school the next morning. At 12 years old, I was hooked.

For all I knew, Carmen could have been a catfish, but the escape into another lifestyle beyond my own was fascinating. Perhaps what mattered most was not so much with whom I was speaking, but that the whom I was speaking with was from somewhere else. Even back then I was captivated by the thought of how something as seemingly insignificant as how we all "spontaneously" spend a Friday night is directly influenced by our external setting. While her Friday nights consisted of controversial, questionable, and potentially made-up events, mine were spent taking the bikes from Aisle 11 and riding laps around Walmart. In my defense, we should realize that none of these completely opposite lifestyles are better than any other, for at the end of the day, any day-to-day setting becomes ordinary and, whether you're Damon or Carmen, what it appears we all seek is a glimpse into how everyone else is spending their time.

The point is that, with the invention of the internet and eventually social media, all it takes is a tap of a finger to be transported in seconds to a real life elsewhere, where we can learn about other people's realities in real time and compare them to our own. The internet has pushed us into a new awareness of exploring what exists beyond our bubbles—something we previously had to rely on others for: mainstream media outlets to broadcast our news, tourism boards to tell us where to travel, a friend-of-a-friend introduces us to their friend-of-a-friend. Now, playlists introduce us to genres and artists from countries we had never considered listening to. Dating apps match us with the potential love of our life from the same country our governments may deem as an enemy. Cities' street views are available for us to walk around virtually. International products, even dinners, can be easily delivered to our doorsteps. Even whole websites can be translated in seconds.

The internet is the best example of something we have that is nationless, the most global of the tools of global citizenship. Although it can easily consume us in ways we had never expected—an omnipresent, comfortable escape from the real world that so often results in mindlessly scrolling down an endless rabbit hole of content—if we learn to be the ones in control of the internet, instead of letting it summon us at the ping of every last notification, we can always remind ourselves that not all connection, neither literally nor figuratively, has been lost.

CHECK-IN

- Would you be fine with having a strictly virtual friend?

- Do you have any current friends you speak with more online than in person?

- Circle the word that applies to you and complete the sentence: When I travel, I am on my phone more/less. I am _____ [fill in with what you are doing].

- What country produces most of the media you consume?

- Which country or countries do you think could grow in global prominence in terms of politics, pop culture, tourism, etc.?

YOU ARE HERE

1. How accurately does your online persona reflect the you in real life?

How much of your real life is spent on your digital persona? For example: taking photos for social media, filming social media stories of fun moments.

_____

_____

_____

_____

_____

_____

_____

2. You've just returned from a trip and realize you don't have any photos or videos to show for it. Do you feel rejuvenated that you lived in the moment or bummed that you have nothing visual to share?

_____

_____

_____

_____

_____

_____

_____

3. You're in charge of the media to unite your country after a disruptive event. What traditional songs do you play over the radio waves, and what comfort shows or movies do you play on public broadcast channels?

Do you, personally, enjoy these?

_____

_____

_____

_____

_____

_____

_____

_____

_____

4. How many hours did you spend in front of a screen today?

Would you say those hours were still well spent even though they were spent virtually? Looking back, when was the last time you went more than a day without looking at a screen of any kind?

_____

_____

_____

_____

_____

_____

_____

_____

5. In terms of technology, in which ways is your country advanced, and in which ways would you say your country is behind?

How easily does your country adopt new technologies? How easily do you adopt new technologies?

6. Looking at your follow list, do you follow anyone—friends or public figures—from another country? Are you followed by anyone from another country?

Does your country produce or import the bulk of its entertainment?

7. You just moved to a country where there is no internet connection. How would your current day-to-day, from work to fun, change? Fill in the 24-hour day schedule.

Would this be even more of a reason to move or a deal breaker for you? How would you feel living without any internet or social media in today's day and age? Do you know anybody who is already living in this way?

12 a.m.		12 p.m.	
1 a.m.		1 p.m.	
2 a.m.		2 p.m.	
3 a.m.		3 p.m.	
4 a.m.		4 p.m.	
5 a.m.		5 p.m.	
6 a.m.		6 p.m.	
7 a.m.		7 p.m.	
8 a.m.		8 p.m.	
9 a.m.		9 p.m.	
10 a.m.		10 p.m.	
11 a.m.		11 p.m.	

8. Has another country's culture seeped into your own, due to proximity or political relationship? For example: Turkish telenovelas in Romania, Spanish lyrics in the American Top 40, Arabic influence on French language.

9. To what extent do you feel that the media should be censored, because of nudity, curse words, violence and so on?

Who should be in control of what's censored? How much "controversial" content have you been exposed to? How has it impacted you? Is it important to be sheltered to some extent or given free rein to express oneself through your choice of media content?

10. How much of your life has been influenced by the internet (e.g. your job, your friends, your love life, your entertainment)? How might this be different had the internet never existed?

Money and career

IF YOU flip to page 8 of the 2005 New Haven Middle School yearbook, you'll find a picture of 14-year-old Damon Dominique, and right underneath, the job title of my dream career I was asked to submit. Looking back years later, what stands out most to me is not only that under my photo you'll find the word "Entrepreneur," but just how representative of American culture it is to sign off one's middle school experience by revealing one's dream career.

As much as my yearbook entry and the American Dream went hand in hand, it has always been crystal clear to me that the traditional American Dream would complicate the lifestyle I wanted to live as a global citizen. For me, the response "Entrepreneur" wasn't about business; it was about freedom. What good would deeply planted roots in one place with an on-location job and a large house do when I preferred to be spontaneous and nomadic? In reality, the goal can include both. It's not that we have to completely abandon the American Dream, but rather be lucid enough to see if it's what we're ultimately wishing to pursue in our lifetime. Today, with the invention of the internet, more and more people are awakening from the American Dream and considering a Global Reality.

This Global Reality is easier said than done no matter which culture you come from. The first obstacle to overcome is one of financial freedom, which at the end of the day still requires the utmost control of one's finances. The second is to understand the reality of how converting your currency in one country may mean you're richer, whereas in another it may mean you're poorer. The truth is: traveling hits certain currencies and therefore certain populations harder. History and international relations have a lot to do with this.

Fitting with the rest of the book, in this chapter we're noticing how our past, present, and future have been and are being influenced by external factors such as how solid our economy is, how strong our currency is, or how promising our job market is. These are often in relation to how everyone else around the world is doing: international supply and demand of our country's resources, market crashes causing years of a recession or inflation, international sanctions and boycotts, and so on and so forth.

On a personal level, these global chess moves boil down to how many taxes are taken out of our paycheck or how widespread a cultural notion like the American Dream even becomes. For some cultures, this peace of mind around financial security does come in the form of high-paying jobs, nice cars, and big homes, whereas for others, peace of mind means not placing all of one's primary life focus on acquiring money and possessions in the first place, as they're subject to rapid change or loss of value. This is why you'll meet some of the happiest people in places around the world that don't have much at all, and some of the most stressed people in places with the most, as well as people whose money and career give their life meaning and people whose money and career get in the way of their life's meaning. Where do you stand?

The aspects that contribute to our answer to this question are aspects that may be commonplace in our culture but are not necessarily fact elsewhere. In other words, these aspects are variables, not constants (and are therefore open to change): daily working hours, the length of the workweek, the minimum wage, average yearly salaries, tax bracket rates, retirement age, laws around incorporating a company, and benefits like health insurance, parental leave, or paid vacation. If the work culture in your country doesn't work for you, try working in another.

CHECK-IN

- How much does (or would) your job/career define your identity?

- When thinking about your current or future career, rank the following in order of importance: money, status, creativity, freedom, social impact, colleagues, and work environment.

- Has your country's financial situation impacted you personally? If so, how?

- To what extent are you aware of your country's wealth or lack thereof in comparison to other countries?

- Someone on the street asks you for money. In the majority of instances, do you give some to them? Why or why not?

YOU ARE HERE

1. Are you working in or toward the field you thought you'd be working in growing up?

How have your parents influenced the career you have/will have? How much family pressure is placed on decisions around money and career? Are you financially responsible for anyone else?

_____

_____

_____

_____

_____

_____

_____

_____

2. In your country, how are the "rich" and "poor" perceived? What lessons can you learn from this?

What is ultimately the end goal for money in your country? A home? Family? Travel?

_____

_____

_____

_____

_____

_____

_____

_____

3. What end goal are you working toward for your money?

Why do you work? What are you ultimately seeking by earning more money? More financial security? Family liabilities?

_____

_____

_____

_____

_____

_____

_____

_____

_____

_____

4. Do you feel you are more financially literate than the average person your age? For example in terms of retirement provision, digital currency, investments, the stock market, etc. Why or why not?

_____

_____

_____

_____

_____

_____

_____

_____

_____

_____

5. You are offered your dream job, but it's located halfway across the world. Your friends and family prefer that you stay home. Explain the thought process leading to your decision.

---

6. In which areas do you find yourself OK with splurging? In which areas do you find yourself OK with skimping? Do you currently live above, below, or within your means?

If $100 was your budget for the week, how does your current spending compare with this?

---

7. In the worst-case scenario where you go bankrupt and lose it all—your job, your house, your everything—what is the first thing you do?

Do you have a financial support system that could help you get back on your feet—for example by sleeping on a friend's couch or borrowing money from parents?

_____

_____

_____

_____

_____

_____

_____

_____

_____

8. Do you make more or less than the people closest to you? How might making more/less affect the dynamic with those around you?

Do you tell others how much money you have and how much you make? Why or why not?

_____

_____

_____

_____

_____

_____

_____

_____

_____

9. You're offered a promotion for more stake and salary in your company, but that requires more of your time. Do you take it? Why/why not?

_____

_____

_____

_____

_____

_____

_____

_____

_____

_____

_____

10. What is the appropriate salary needed to meet your ideal lifestyle in your ideal country?

_____

_____

_____

_____

_____

_____

_____

_____

_____

_____

Beauty and body

LET'S START with the naked truth about how we came into this world: naked. Within minutes, we're covered up and will stay that way until we die, when even then we remain clothed. Initially, the purpose of clothing was to provide warmth and protection, but over thousands of years of civilization, humans have developed it into industries and art forms called fashion and beauty, where many of us now try to keep up with the ins and outs of what's in and what's out. What's more, when you travel, you'll notice what was in is now out and what was out is now in.

After a trip to Brazil, where I learned that the common female swimsuit was referred to as a "dental floss bikini" in Portuguese, it clicked for me that, although I'm from the depths of Indiana where even wearing board shorts above the knee is reason enough to get a second look, I was no longer in Indiana and no longer needed to adhere to Midwestern cultural standards. The next day I bought my first *sunga* (the type of Speedo many Brazilian men wear). When I asked the store clerk if it "looked OK," she confirmed, going so far as to say that anything else from now on would "feel like an adult diaper." I bought it and for the first time in my life discovered the intense pain of a thigh sunburn.

My next culture shock came in the form of reverse culture shock when the pool attendant at my Hollywood gym denied me entry because I needed to wear a swimsuit. I was wearing the same Brazilian *sunga*.

As global citizens, we will be, for lack of a better word, exposed to many of these cultural norms that are relative only to their place in the world. Your opinions and judgments of how much skin you show, where you show it, who can show it, in which age range it's appropriate to show it, how much of it you decorate with tattoos or piercings, and how much body hair you keep or trim off, have all been, and are still being, influenced by your surroundings. Factors like religion, which might dictate one's morality or vanity scale, or the pop culture at the time, which might inform you of the latest makeup or fashion trend, are all at play internally when it comes down to even our most minor casual behaviors: whether you feel awkward or confident changing your shirt in a room with others, how you would dress or do your makeup when meeting your friends versus meeting your partner's parents, and if you're the type to take 50 photos to get one good one or post the first one you got.

Understanding that such external influences are not ubiquitous is key in reclaiming our own self-esteem; once placed in another cultural context and subject to another set of beauty and body standards, how we feel about ourselves could completely change.

Now that we can identify the pattern of these external influences on our inner state (which then contribute to our outward expression), we can notice when we are only trying to adhere to a set of ever-fleeting standards, that our genetics are a luck of the draw, and that our culture's interpretation of them in the generation we're alive is even more so. It would be a shame to base our entire image of ourselves on our body— something that is more or less unchangeable—when we could focus it on something that is changeable: our mind.

CHECK-IN

- Which part of your physical appearance do you take the most care of, if any at all? For example: hairstyle, wrinkles, body fat, muscles.

- How much awareness do you have of hygiene or beauty traditions around the world?

- What habits do you have that others might find unattractive?

- You have no one to see, nowhere to go. Do you still get dressed as you typically would?

- What has had the greatest influence on your current relationship with your beauty and body?

YOU ARE HERE

1. The airline lost your luggage with all your favorite, most-used hygiene products. What is your game plan now?

_____

_____

_____

_____

_____

_____

_____

_____

2. You just noticed a wrinkle you had never had before. How do you react?

As you grow older, do you feel more or less comfortable with your body? How are aging and older people perceived in your culture? Are you as excited for your older years as you are/ were for your youth?

_____

_____

_____

_____

_____

_____

_____

_____

3. Which public figures in your culture are heralded as being the most beautiful? Where are they from and what features define them?

_____

_____

_____

_____

_____

_____

_____

_____

_____

_____

4. You're sitting for a caricaturist. Which aspect of your physical appearance do you think they would most focus on? Now draw the caricature.

Is this an aspect of yourself you accentuate or cover up? How much is what you accentuate/cover up influenced by your society's general ideas of beauty?

5. You wake up in a different body. How might you present yourself differently with this new body knowing your old one still exists as well? Consider fashion, hairstyles, body hair, tattoos and piercings, and so on.

Why, in reality, don't you present yourself more like this new body? Where did your current style and grooming routine originate?

_____

_____

_____

_____

_____

_____

_____

_____

6. What do you find ugly?

What styles in terms of beauty or fashion would you never take on? Why not? Is your culture's general idea of beauty more aligned with decorating the body with adornment (tattoos, piercings, makeup, etc.) or keeping it as natural as possible?

_____

_____

_____

_____

_____

_____

_____

_____

7. What is your relationship with your own body and how much others see?

You show up to a nudist beach in Germany. How much are you willing to undress? Would you wear a Speedo? Go topless at a beach? Take off your shirt at the gym? Send a nude picture? Sleep without pajamas?

_____

_____

_____

_____

_____

_____

_____

_____

_____

_____

8. Your wallet was just found in a Berlin coffee shop and someone is providing a written description of you—your style and your look—for the barista. Write their description of you from their perspective.

_____

_____

_____

_____

_____

_____

_____

_____

_____

9. How might your natural look or current body shape be accepted in another country or culture? Where in the world would you feel more attractive?

10. To what extent are you willing to modify your looks? For example: teeth whitening strips, braces, tanning, Lasik, piercing, tattoos, investing in high-quality skin care, plastic surgery.

Who or what do you think has influenced your decision around the extent you're willing to go?

Food and drink

IF YOU were to pick up a random travel magazine or binge any given travel show, you'd probably learn mostly about what world cultures are eating, how they're eating, and where the ever-changing trendy restaurants are located to be eating it. And while I do enjoy a generous pour of Merlot, a spicy Thai green curry, or a velvety flat white—and honestly, if the offer were extended, I would probably enjoy them all at once—I admit I've never been much of a foodie, nor a meat eater, and thus my food encounters around the world have been frequent and awkward.

For starters, tipping etiquette around the world is complicated. As if it's not already difficult enough to decipher how the local currency converts to in one's home currency, we then have to decipher what an appropriate tipping percentage is too, or if there even is a tipping culture. Next, being vegetarian around the world often means the vegetarian special you've ordered turns out to be either a bowl of lettuce leaves or some heavy sauce with a side of lentils. Lastly, you have the adorable families who don't care what your eating habits are, as long as you just keep eating. Plate after plate until you can barely breathe, and then out comes Abuelita Yolanda from her kitchen in Quito, Ecuador, with yet another plate. Delicious, yes, but enough, Yolanda!

When we talk about topics like food and drink, we're also having a sideline conversation about another: manners. Refusing food, not blessing each other before a meal with a "Bon appétit," and excusing oneself from someone else's dinner table may come across as rude in one culture, just as eating with elbows on the table and slurping one's soup would in mine. While breaking these unspoken rules may give some people the impression we're being rude when we don't mean to be, we as global citizens can now recognize them for what they are: innocent manners that probably work within a different context. For instance, when many Europeans have finished eating at fast food restaurants in the US, they often leave their trays on their table because that's how it's done in Europe. The busser comes around and scoffs at how people could be so rude! Then that same American busser goes to Europe and waits patiently as the grocery store cashier rings up his groceries, resulting in an angry cashier wondering why he hasn't started bagging his own groceries, which is customary in Europe.

It's not just about manners in terms of behavior around the food, but where we draw the lines on what is acceptable to eat. In Ljubljana, Slovenia, eating a burger made from horse meat is nothing that would surprise a Slovenian; it was only the tourists who were shocked and who ordered a regular beef burger shortly thereafter. A few thousand miles east of Slovenia, in the Middle East or South Asia, beef or pork might be the animal meats you must avoid at all costs, either because a culture considers an animal unclean (as the pig is in Islamic or Jewish cultures) or sacred (as the cow is in Hinduism).

To me, what's most interesting about cuisines around the world is not exactly the food itself, but the establishments. Hunger is rather fleeting, but the people and places making the food are not. The person selling roasted corn on the street corner is just as much a mental image of what Mexican culture stands for as the roasted corn on the cob itself. This is the case for the old-fashioned diner in the US, the teahouse in Japan, the juice bar in Brazil, and the pretzel stand in

Romania. These vendors, their stands, and the communities around them add to the visual component of our cities and therefore, cultures.

So, does our hunger for travel ultimately stem from our hunger for new foods? Or are we thirsting for another side of the travel industry?

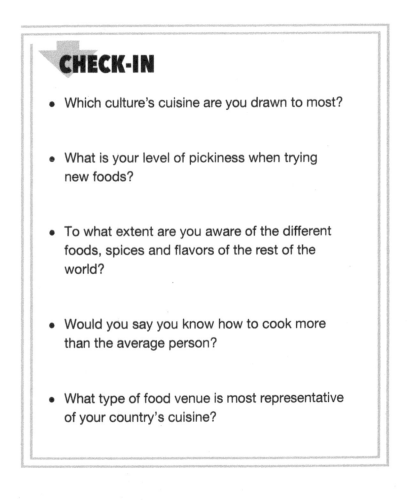

CHECK-IN

- Which culture's cuisine are you drawn to most?

- What is your level of pickiness when trying new foods?

- To what extent are you aware of the different foods, spices and flavors of the rest of the world?

- Would you say you know how to cook more than the average person?

- What type of food venue is most representative of your country's cuisine?

YOU ARE HERE

1. Looking at yesterday, write down what you ate, and the times you ate it:

Are these foods and meal times representative of the culture you're most familiar with?

_____

_____

_____

_____

_____

_____

_____

_____

_____

_____

2. A friend is writing your grocery list. What food staples easily identify you and definitely make the list every time?

-

-

-

-

-

3. You are in charge of your country's upcoming drinking and drug law reform. Reflect on the current legislature, and the potential laws you would most support or reject.

What is your and your closest friends' relationship with alcohol and other substances? Consider the drinking age, drinking in public, legality of substances and so on.

_____

_____

_____

_____

_____

_____

_____

_____

_____

_____

4. Financially, you're scraping by. What foods are the cheapest foods to eat where you are from?

_____

_____

_____

_____

_____

_____

_____

_____

_____

_____

_____

5. You're in charge of cooking your favorite family recipe for a friend from out of town. What do you cook? Why?

Does your culture have a traditional meal used for ceremonies or celebrations?

_____

_____

_____

_____

_____

_____

_____

_____

_____

_____

6. You just got fired, broke off your engagement, and your dog died. It's time to eat. What are your go-to comfort foods? What about them do you find comforting in times of stress or grief?

Do you think you'd be able to find these abroad?

_____

_____

_____

_____

_____

_____

_____

_____

_____

_____

7. Would it be more acceptable to tell your friends you ate macaroni and cheese with a soda, or a kale salad with kombucha?

Why? How much of an influence does nutrition and health have on your daily eating habits?

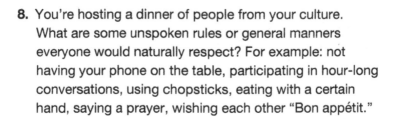

8. You're hosting a dinner of people from your culture. What are some unspoken rules or general manners everyone would naturally respect? For example: not having your phone on the table, participating in hour-long conversations, using chopsticks, eating with a certain hand, saying a prayer, wishing each other "Bon appétit."

9. From another country's perspective, how would you say your culture's cuisine is perceived?

_____

_____

_____

_____

_____

_____

_____

_____

_____

_____

10. A friend from another country just opened your fridge. What food combinations might they find odd? For example: mixing ketchup and cheese together, eating sardines straight from the can.

_____

_____

_____

_____

_____

_____

_____

_____

_____

_____

_____

_____

Travel and the world

IT'S NO secret that a global citizen's weakness is also their strength: traveling. If there's one thing in this world we're actually attached to, it's booking another trip before the current one is over and questioning if the place we're visiting could potentially be the one we call home one day. As a strength, this insatiable desire to travel offers us an endless array of ways to occupy our time and keep us interested in the present and future. As a weakness, we're constantly operating with a "Could the grass be greener on the other side?" mentality, paradoxically feeling very present, and yet curiously wondering what could be lying just around the corner.

You see, to outsiders, when they see someone traveling, it appears to them that they're traveling to see the world. Maybe that's even what you think. But that's the obvious answer. Rather, isn't it almost always the case that when we return from a trip and someone asks, "So how was it?" the stories we then recount are ones about what happened in and around the beautiful locations rather than about the beautiful locations themselves? In other words, while we're undoubtedly seeking exotic destinations we're not familiar with, more accurately, we're seeking adventures that serve as reminders that our life is happening now. For instance, off the top of my head, I can't tell you the name or location of the highly recommended Thai waterfall I went to, or even tell you much about how beautiful it was, but I can tell you exactly how alive I felt when my friend and I hurriedly climbed up the rocky path to catch the sunset atop the waterfall with tourists and locals alike, only to return to our $5 motorbike rental with a dead iPhone and no GPS to guide us through the jungle at nightfall. Spoiler: we were never happier to stop at a 7/11 gas station to ask the cashier for directions in butchered Thai. In theory, this waterfall, jungle, or 7/11 could have been replaced by any other city, beach, or famous landmark, because, despite what we might tell ourselves, our travels are never about sightseeing, but rather about the stories that come from the sights.

You see, upon our departure, it's the waterfalls and jungles we think we're intrigued by, but upon our arrival back home, it's the adventures set around them. The exact details about the waterfalls and jungle are almost never as captivating as the juicy date we went on with the Uber driver, the night we won the bar's trivia competition when we don't even speak Spanish, or the awkward moment when we had to convince the driver to pull the public bus over because we were feeling sick. Why? Because these stories not only remind you of your eventful life, but also allow the listener to see themselves in your experience—what it would be like if they, too, went there.

Because travel places us in another setting that's unlike the one we're used to, our eyes are open wider toward life. This is unlike our day-to-day realities back home where we observe life through our own one-dimensional lens set in a narrative we've grown accustomed to: the routines. When we're completely in control of the direction of the narrative, the status quo, the experience doesn't always feel as vivid or stimulating as when it's being questioned in contexts outside the one we're used to. It's not that these exciting stories can't happen at home; it's that some are so used to their usual routines and preferences that they think they already know how every last adventure could pan out. To them, there are no mysterious secrets or dramatic plotlines for their place in the world; they think these only exist elsewhere ... and that's why, for them, they do.

Though a global lifestyle checking off waterfalls and jungles requires time and money, the global citizen mindset is always free.

It felt fitting to end *You Are A Global Citizen* with this "Travel and the world" chapter, not because it's revolving around the most obvious aspect in becoming a global citizen, but because, as ironic as it may sound, I believe it's often everything else in your life that makes up who you are—the conditioning of your "Origins," everything abstract going on "Internally," and all the constant "External" forces at play—and finally, it's the travel that points it out to you. It appears, to me at least, that the experiences from our travels resonate most vividly because unbeknown to us in the moment, they're stimulating something that already exists in us: a facet of our identity that is now being challenged or a facet that is now being solidified. We tend to instinctively correlate our transformative travels with the evolution of our self, but we seldom give much thought to how that moment was revolutionary because it pointed out or changed something in us that was already there. That "something in us that was already there" was every chapter before this one.

And now finally, we need this one to realize it.

CHECK-IN

- What country, other than your own, would you say you know the most about?

- If you were presented with the outlines of a world map, how confidently could you fill it in with country names?

- When you have nothing to do, do you spend the majority of your time at home or out and about?

- What places consistently treat you well and do you have a good time in?

- What, or where, makes you feel most alive?

YOU ARE HERE

1. In this map of the world, label the places you've traveled to. Add a star to the places you liked most and cross out the places you liked least. Now shade in the places you'd like to visit. Is there a pattern you notice?

2. You've received an opportunity to embark upon a three-month trip around the world, and then learn it's a solo trip. Would you still do it? Describe how you'd feel.

3. Where do most people around you travel to? For the weekend? For vacation? If they were to relocate within your country? If they were to relocate outside your country?

4. The ten-year-old version of yourself asks if you've been to all your childhood dream destinations. Where were these dream destinations and if you've been, were they as magical as you had once hoped?

Where are you currently dreaming about? How do you feel now that you have seen the places you have always wanted to see in the world? Does the world feel smaller or bigger?

5. Would you still travel to a country that, on a government level, wouldn't support you? For example: LGBTQ+ rights, racial or gender discrimination.

_____

_____

_____

_____

_____

_____

_____

_____

_____

_____

_____

6. Who in your life has led you to a certain destination? Have you been the reason somebody else has traveled somewhere?

_____

_____

_____

_____

_____

_____

_____

_____

_____

_____

_____

7. In what ways might someone experience culture shock in your home country?

_____

_____

_____

_____

_____

_____

_____

_____

_____

_____

8. What advantages does your region or country offer you in terms of being able to relocate elsewhere (whether national territories or foreign countries) with minimal restrictions? For example: EU citizens moving within the Schengen Area, Americans moving to Puerto Rico.

_____

_____

_____

_____

_____

_____

_____

_____

_____

_____

9. Based on your knowledge and experience, where would and wouldn't you recommend people travel to and why?

Recommended	Not recommended

10. After finishing this book, do you now feel closer or farther away from the culture you're most familiar with? How does this make you feel?

_____

_____

_____

_____

_____

_____

_____

_____

_____

_____

_____

_____

Final reflections

NOW THAT we can identify a link between the culture we are most familiar with that made us into the person we are most familiar with, we can reflect on the following, final questions.

Which cultural patterns are you now aware you embody?

_____

_____

_____

_____

_____

_____

_____

What surprising cultural realizations have come about from
working through this book?

_____

_____

_____

_____

_____

_____

_____

Which parts of your culture do you admire and appreciate
most?

_____

_____

_____

_____

_____

_____

_____

Which parts of your culture are you now more critical of?

_____

_____

_____

_____

_____

_____

_____

Note any further observations or reminders for yourself
you'd like to remember down the line about this adventure
of becoming a global citizen.

_____

_____

_____

_____

_____

_____

_____

Now compare your answers with the ones you wrote in
"First reflections." What do you notice?

_____

_____

_____

_____

_____

_____

_____

A final note

THIS ISN'T a guidebook for a specific destination, but one for the only destination that is always there no matter where you go: you. I hope that the questions in this book have shed light on the ways in which your behavior and current outlook of the world could have been influenced solely by the culture in which you happened to be born, and equally to what extent these either hinder or further you in the direction you want to go from here. With this insight, we are all now one step closer to unloading, unpacking, and reorganizing not only our own baggage, but also that of the world.

Congratulations. You are a global citizen.

Acknowledgments

THROUGHOUT MY travels, what I believed I was always searching for were the foreign destinations, but what I found most life-altering were the people. Global Citizen people.

The first person I want to acknowledge is the first person I ever fell in love with: Solal, whom I met on International Night at a club in Paris—six hours of dancing that turned into six years of a relationship and now a long-lasting bond. I was 19, abroad, anonymous, and drunk on bottom-shelf wine when the Sia lyric "I'm bulletproof, nothing to lose, fire away, fire away" filled the dance floor and probably for the first time, I truly felt alive. I was attracted to him because he proved every gay stereotype wrong and wasn't looking for anyone else's approval or disapproval about it. Over the course of our mostly long-distance relationship, he expanded my view of the world, and myself, by constantly questioning, teasing, and provoking my Americanness.

Next, I must say cheers to my British assistant, Chloe, who is one of the only people I have met who can articulate this exhausting, yet exciting philosophical deep-dive that, on the bright side, helped me to write this book. Perhaps this insight was possible because she, too, lived abroad in Paris.

I must also thank Fran, my American manager living in Paris, as well as Emma and Sarah of this very book publisher who I met years ago in London, for understanding the good, bad, and ugly of a life around the world and also believing a book should be made about it.

At the end of the day, nothing can happen without people. So thank you, *merci, gracias, danke, obrigado, grazie, shukran*, and all the other languages of the people I have, and have not yet met—and to the whoever, the whatever, or possibly even the nothing that made it so that we were all where we were, when we were, and who we were.